Strategic Japan

Strategic Japan

New Approaches to Foreign
Policy and the U.S.-Japan
Alliance

Editors
Michael J. Green
Zack Cooper

CSIS | CENTER FOR STRATEGIC &
INTERNATIONAL STUDIES

ROWMAN & LITTLEFIELD
Lanham • Boulder • New York • Toronto • Plymouth, UK

Center for Strategic & International Studies
1616 Rhode Island Avenue, NW
Washington, DC 20036
202-887-0200 | www.csis.org

Rowman & Littlefield
A wholly owned subsidiary of The Rowman & Littlefield
Publishing Group, Inc.
4501 Forbes Boulevard, Suite 200, Lanham, Maryland 20706
www.rowman.com

Unit A, Whitacre Mews, 26-34 Stannery Street, London SE11 4AB

ISBN: 978-1-4422-2863-4 (hb)
ISBN: 978-1-4422-2864-1 (pbk)
ISBN: 978-1-4422-2865-8 (electronic)

Contents

1. Introduction | *Michael J. Green*   I

2. How to Understand China's Assertiveness since 2009:   7
   Hypotheses and Policy Implications | *Yasuhiro Matsuda*

3. U.S.-Japan Allied Maritime Strategy: Balancing the   35
   Rise of Maritime China | *Tetsuo Kotani*

4. Japan's North Korea Strategy: Dealing with New   61
   Challenges | *Hiroyasu Akutsu*

5. Enhancing Energy Resilience: Challenging Tasks for   79
   Japan's Energy Policy | *Yoshikazu Kobayashi*

6. Japan's Strategy toward Southeast Asia and the   III
   Japan-U.S. Alliance | *Nobuhiro Aizawa*

Index   129

About the Authors   141

About CSIS
                                                                                        143

1. INTRODUCTION

Michael J. Green

Does Japan have a grand strategy? Is Japan capable of grand strategy? In the early postwar period Japanese Prime Minister Shigeru Yoshida established a path for Japan to reestablish its position internationally through a brilliant grand strategy. He aligned with the United States but steadily rebuilt Japanese freedom of action in Asia while focusing on economic revitalization. In the first five decades after the war, Japan produced few strategists but many highly talented tacticians in the halls of the Ministry of Finance and in the manufacturing sector of the economy. With the collapse of Japan's economic bubble and the rise of a willful and unpredictable China, Japan has had to search for new tools of statecraft to preserve autonomy and prestige in an often-unforgiving hierarchical power structure in Asia. Prime Minister Shinzo Abe has garnered attention for his policy of "proactive pacifism," but in fact many of Abe's initiatives build on those of his immediate predecessor, Yoshihiko Noda of the Democratic Party of Japan, as well as previous leaders from the Liberal Democratic Party.

Abe's revisions to the Yoshida Doctrine come in two areas that Yoshida himself probably anticipated would arise eventually. First, Abe is focused on rebuilding Japan's economic strength through the three arrows of his "Abenomics," which consists of fiscal stimulus, quantitative easing, and restructuring. Although the last of these three arrows will be the most difficult, Japan's successful completion of Trans-Pacific Partnership negotiations would reinforce it. In addition, Abe is enhancing Japan's indigenous power by realigning national security institutions, including the establishment of a new National Security Council (NSC) and the relaxation of the government's bans on collective self-defense and arms exports. These aspects of "internal balancing" are being matched by new "external balancing" efforts—primarily through alignment with other maritime and democratic states wary of China's growing assertiveness. The United States and Japan are revising their bilateral Defense Guidelines and Abe is building on security agreements with India and Australia while developing new ties with the Philippines and other countries in the Association of Southeast Asian Nations (ASEAN). The glaring hole in Abe's external balancing strategy is the Republic of Korea (ROK), where historic animosities have reemerged to confound the two democratic neighbors' bilateral ties.

Shaping this new strategy is a generation of Japanese scholars and foreign policy experts who came of age in the post–Cold War era. Trained in the West but fluent in Asian languages, they are poised to take positions of influence as decisionmaking is increasingly centralized in the Prime Minister's Office and the new NSC.

The Center for Strategic and International Studies (CSIS) invited five of these experts to be short-term visiting scholars in Washington, D.C., during the first quarter of 2014, where they partnered with CSIS counterparts to produce strategy memos on their geographic and functional areas of expertise. The purpose of this initiative was to enlighten the American policy debate on an array of topics related to Japan and the broader Asia Pacific, broaden the visiting fellows' personal networks in Washington, and help them hone their arguments for policymakers in both the United States and Japan.

I would like to thank CSIS fellow Zack Cooper for his central role in assisting the visiting scholars with securing meetings, revising their papers, and organizing policy roundtables. The project also hinged on the visiting scholars' collaboration with CSIS and Washington-based counterparts, who generously shared their contacts, ideas, and time. I would also like to thank Will Colson, Lara Crouch, Mary Popeo, James Dunton, and Ali Bours for their assistance in bringing this final product together.

Yasuhiro Matsuda of the University of Tokyo seeks to explain China's assertiveness since 2009 and to outline a joint American and Japanese strategic response. He presents three hypotheses for explaining Chinese behavior: the rising power trend (that China's assertiveness will only grow with its power), cycles of deterioration/amelioration (that improved or deteriorated foreign relations are largely determined by economic conditions and leadership dynamics in China), and strategic rivalry (that China manages its security environment such that it always has only one external rival). Matsuda explains how all three elements are at play simultaneously and recommends that the United States be more engaged in Asia and that regional states like Japan seek opportunities to improve relations with China while holding firm against its coercive measures. Dr. Matsuda worked with Chris Johnson and Bonnie Glaser of the Freeman Chair in China Studies at CSIS to complete this paper.

Tetsuo Kotani of the Japan Institute of International Affairs examines China's maritime strategy and possible responses by Japan and the United States. After assessing the doctrinal debate in the United States, he argues that the United States and Japan can deter China from using force in the First Island Chain because a war at sea would choke off China's sea lanes. However, he also cautions that deterrence through war-winning capabilities is not enough and that the United States and Japan will have to develop new capabilities, plans, and operational concepts to address non-kinetic "gray zone" scenarios involving Chinese coercion. Mr. Kotani worked with Wallace "Chip" Gregson (Ltgen, USMC, Ret.) of the Center for the National Interest and T. X. Hammes (Col, USMC, Ret.) of the National Defense University's Institute for National Security Studies.

Hiroyasu Akutsu of the National Institute for Defense Studies explains Japan's emerging North Korea strategy, highlighting the importance of American and Japanese trilateral cooperation with the ROK and the need for Japan and the ROK to increase bilateral security cooperation. He also explores strategies to deter North Korean provocations and proliferation, such as addressing the right of collective self-defense and enhancing ballistic missile defense. Dr. Akutsu worked with CSIS Korea Chair Victor Cha.

Yoshikazu Kobayashi of the Institute of Energy Economics, Japan presents a strategy for enhancing energy resilience in the wake of the March 11, 2011, earthquake, tsunami, and nuclear disaster in northern Japan. While noting that resilience requires improving the nation's resistance to hardships and shock, elasticity to mitigate impacts of such events, and robustness to achieve prompt recovery, Kobayashi argues that Japan's current policy focuses disproportionately on risk mitigation to prevent energy crises at the expense of mitigation and emergency response and recovery once such an event has occurred. He provides recommendations that address all three pillars of energy resilience: diversification of fossil fuel sources, acknowledgment of energy supply risks, additional stockpiling, adaptive regulatory structures, and increasing government response capacity through exercises. Mr. Kobayashi worked with David Pumphrey and Jane Nakano of the CSIS Energy and National Security Program.

Nobuhiro Aizawa of Kyushu University writes about the importance of Southeast Asia to Japan's regional strategy and economic future. He focuses on Japan's role in assisting ASEAN states with sustainable economic and political development and security resilience. He argues that Japan can play a larger role by providing economic support and guidance to the region, offering a model of good governance and democracy, acting as a standard-setter for disaster response, and facilitating intra-regional cooperation for the security of the air and maritime domains. Dr. Aizawa worked with Ernest Bower and Murray Hiebert of the CSIS Sumitro Chair for Southeast Asian Studies.

Taken together, these five essays highlight areas for enhanced cooperation between the United States and Japan at a time when the United States needs a confident and proactive Japan, and Japan needs sustained American engagement and deterrence in a changing Asia Pacific region. ▪

2. HOW TO UNDERSTAND CHINA'S ASSERTIVENESS SINCE 2009: HYPOTHESES AND POLICY IMPLICATIONS

Yasuhiro Matsuda

> *Since the establishment of diplomatic relations with us, the Japanese government and its leaders have repeatedly made it clear in public that Japan's war with China was an act of aggression and that Japan expressed its deep, sincere apology toward the countries it invaded. The government and the people of China give this record positive evaluation.... China's economic reform and modernization benefited from support by the government and the people of Japan. The people of China will long remember it.*
>
> —Wen Jiabao's address to the National Diet of Japan, April 12, 2007[1]

> *It is easier to forgive an enemy than to forgive a friend.*
>
> —William Blake

---

1. The excerpt is an English translation. The Chinese original text and Japanese translation are available at Akihiko Tanaka, "The World and Japan," Database Project, Institute for Advanced Studies on Asia, University of Tokyo, http://www.ioc.u-tokyo.ac.jp/~worldjpn/documents/texts/JPCH/20070412.S1C.html and http://www.ioc.u-tokyo.ac.jp/~worldjpn/documents/texts/JPCH/20070412.S1J.html.

INTRODUCTION

No nation in the world today has worked more strenuously than Japan to make sense of "China's assertiveness." Much has changed in the Sino-Japanese relationship since Wen Jiabao's 2007 speech, excerpted above. Within these seven years, the Chinese government's perceptions of Japan have transformed. Japan is viewed as a nation perilously tilting toward or reverting to pre–World War II militarism; a country that never learned the "lessons" of its early twentieth-century history; and a country that actively challenges the status quo in the postwar world order. China has, in turn, reacted with diplomatic and political pressure on Japan. Of course, China's claim that Japan precipitously regresses toward the status quo ante remains to be seen.

On the other hand, many scholars have studied China's recent acts of assertiveness, particularly since 2008 and especially in the field of maritime expansion. Michael Swaine and M. Taylor Fravel define Chinese "assertiveness" as Chinese official or governmental behavior and statements that appear to threaten U.S. and allied interests or otherwise challenge the status quo in maritime Asia along China's periphery, thereby undermining Asian stability and causing concern to U.S. and other Asian leaders. They argue that subordinate governmental actors and assertive actions-reactions influenced Beijing's assertive behavior. Andrew Scobell and Scott W. Harold argue that China's assertiveness since 2008 was amplified by two domestic challenges: Chinese leaders' hypersensitivity to popular nationalism and poor bureaucratic coordination among an expanding number of foreign policy actors. The International Crisis Group raises the notion of "reactive assertiveness," which means exploiting "perceived" provocations by other countries in disputed areas to change the status quo in its favor.[2] On the other hand, Alastair Iain Johnston argues that seven events in 2010, which are usually perceived to represent a new assertiveness in Chinese foreign policy, actually demonstrate previous patterns of Chinese assertiveness or China's desire to uphold the status quo on a particular issue, with the exception of China's behavior regarding the South China Sea.

This paper argues cautiously that China's assertiveness is indeed reactive. Countries like Japan, the largest status quo state in the region, would not necessarily need to react vigorously to other nations' "provocations." China does so because it is the biggest rising revisionist state in the region. Japan is the most mature democracy in Asia, and as a result of the freedom of speech it guarantees, discourse on both extremes of the ideological spectrum exists. China seems to "cherry-pick" from either extreme to fit its strategic intent and paint these extremes as predominant in general political Japanese discourse.

It is important to note that Japan is not the only Asian nation subject to China's strategic framing. A similar situation can be observed in China's relations with Vietnam, the Philippines, and Taiwan, all of which are China's neighbors with maritime zones contiguous with those of China.

What explains these countries' deteriorating relations with China? Björn Jerdén argues that "China's new assertiveness existed only as a social fact within the bounds of the inter-

2. Michael Swaine and M. Taylor Fravel, "China's Assertive Behavior, Part Two: The Maritime Periphery," *China Leadership Monitor*, no. 35 (September 21, 2011), http://media.hoover.org/sites/default/files/documents/ CLM35MS.pdf; Andrew Scobell and Scott W. Harold, "An 'Assertive' China? Insights from Interviews," *Asian Security* 9, no. 2 (2013); Alastair Iain Johnston, "How New and Assertive Is China's New Assertiveness?," *International Security* 37, no. 4 (Spring 2013); Dingding Chen, Xiaoyu Pu, and Alastair Iain Johnston, "Debating China's Assertiveness," *International Security* 38, no. 3 (Winter 2013/14); International Crisis Group, "Dangerous Waters: China-Japan Relations on the Rocks," *Asia Report*, no. 245 (April 8, 2013), i, 12–15, http://www.crisisgroup.org/~/media/Files/asia/north-east-asia/245-dangerous-waters-china-japan-relations-on-the-rocks.pdf.

subjective knowledge of a particular discourse, and not as an objectively true phenomenon external to this discourse." He thinks that the assertive narrative since 2009 is wrong; rather, it is U.S. rebalancing policy that triggered China's reaction.[3] This argument suggests that neighbors of China take a hardline approach to China. This hypothesis is hard to sustain, however, because it rests on the assumption that Chinese diplomacy remains "soft," while other states have become hardline without much provocation. It is believed widely that China's diplomatic strategy has taken on a hardline tone, given recent behavior. Why is this so? This paper offers three hypotheses that contribute to explaining China's assertiveness: 1) a "rising trend" hypothesis; 2) a "cycle of deterioration and amelioration" hypothesis; and 3) a "redefinition of strategic rivals" hypothesis. The next three sections discuss each of these three hypotheses, followed by policy implications. Finally, the paper offers some concluding thoughts.

"RISING TREND" HYPOTHESIS

The "rising trend" hypothesis holds that China is becoming more willing to challenge the current political order in Asia by relying on the sheer power of its increased military and economic capabilities. This hypothesis suggests that the turning point for this trend was roughly 2009, when China began to discuss reframing its diplomatic strategy by using the expression "core interests."[4] The 2008 global financial crisis showed the pitfalls of the "Washington consensus" and seemed to vindicate the "Beijing consensus," especially due to China's relatively quick recovery. This greatly emboldened the Chinese

---

3. Björn Jerdén, "The Assertive China Narrative: Why It Is Wrong and How So Many Still Bought into It," *The Chinese Journal of International Politics*, (2014), http://cjip.oxfordjournals.org/content/7/1/47.full.pdf+html.
4. Hiroko Maeda, *Chugoku niokeru Kokueki Ronso to Kakusinteki Rieki* [Debate on National Interest and Core Interest in China], *PHP Policy Review* 6, no. 48 (February 2, 2012): 3–9, http://research.php.co.jp/policyreview/vol6no48.php.

ruling elite, inducing a behavioral shift that became manifest in 2009–10.[5] In addition, China surpassed Japan to become the world's second-largest economy in 2010.

The "rise of China" are widely used buzzwords in both academia and policy circles. The numbers are hard to deny: China's gross domestic product (GDP) quadrupled in the first decade of the new millennium. Great powers have inextricably deepened their economic ties with China. This growth trend is even more pronounced in the military dimension. At the 2014 National People's Congress, Chinese authorities announced that the defense budget would increase by 12.2 percent, while the economic growth target would be 7.5 percent.[6] China's defense budget has increased by double digits every year since 1989, except for 2010.

The Chinese government has also invested in the cultivation of patriotism (*aiguozhuyi*). Figure 1, comprising two graphs, demonstrates one measurable indicator of this initiative; it shows the frequency of references to the words "patriotism (*aiguozhuyi*)" and the "Diaoyu Islands *(Diaoyudao)*" (known as the Senkaku Islands in Japanese) that appeared in both the text and headlines of articles from 1950 to 2010 in the *People's Daily*, the official newspaper for the Communist Party of China. The graphs show a spike around 2009 and 2010 in coverage of both terms, as well as several previous spikes. While not represented on these graphs, it is interesting to note that "internationalism" was stressed more than "patriotism" in its coverage prior to the reform and opening period that began in 1978.

The Chinese government previously used the Japanese label for the Senkaku (or Sento) Islands and regarded them as part of

5. Edward N. Luttwak, *The Rise of China vs. the Logic of Strategy* (Cambridge, MA: Belknap Press of Harvard University Press, 2012), 8.
6. Edward Wong, "China Announces 12.2% Increase in Military Budget," *New York Times*, March 5, 2014, http://www.nytimes.com/2014/03/06/world/asia/china-military-budget.html?partner=rssnyt&emc=rss&_r=1.

the Okinawan island chain.[7] The present-day "historical issues" between Japan and China began in the early 1970s when China started to question Japan's position on the Senkaku Islands and increased in the 1980s with the growth of Chinese nationalism. Figure 1 suggests that the state-led invocation of patriotism began in the 1980s, during which the legitimacy of socialism had begun to erode. This trend became more visible in the wake of the Tiananmen Square incident that took place in June 1989.[8] Following the late 1990s, the frequency of "patriotism" and the "Diaoyu Islands"' use has been a covariate.

Figure 2 captures the concomitant behavior change, especially after 2008, in terms of the frequency of Chinese incursions into the territorial waters of the Senkaku Islands, as well as the frequency of Chinese naval vessels crossing the Ryukyu Islands. Previously, the Chinese government's activities in the East China Sea were guided by a more moderate rationale. This rationale was straightforward: If China attempted to change the status quo, it would have to confront not only Japan but also the United States. Thus, challenges to the status quo were highly likely to increase Sino-U.S. enmity, and therefore be detrimental.

---

7. It is well known that the Chinese government understood that the Senkaku Islands were part of the Ryukyu (or Okinawan) island chain, as demonstrated by *People's Daily*'s reports, declassified Chinese diplomatic archives, and official maps before 1970. "Liuqiu qundao renmin fandui Meiguo zhanling de douzheng" [Ryukyu People's Struggle against U.S. Occupation], *People's Daily*, January 8, 1953. "Tainichiwayaku niokeru ryodobubun no shucho nikansuru yoko soan" [Draft of Guidelines on Issues and Claims of Territories in Peace Treaty with Japan], *Jiji Press*, December 27, 2012. "Chugoku chizu ni'Chogyotou' mikisai: 71 nen izen, Senkaku jikokuryo to minasazu, kokkyosen mo henko" [No Diaoyu Islands on Chinese Maps before 1971: China Sees Them as Foreign Territories and Border Line on the Map Changes after 1971], *Jiji Press*, December 29, 2013.
8. Keiji Kinoshita, "Aikokushugi Kyoiku" [Patriotic Education], in *Kiro ni Tatsu Nittyukankei*, kaiteiban [Sino-Japanese Relations at the Cross-Roads, rev. ed.], ed. Ryoko Iechida et al. (Kyoto: Koyo Shobo, 2013).

Figure 1. Frequency of the Words "Patriotism (aiguozhuyi)" and the "Diaoyu Islands (Diaoyudao)" in the People's Daily

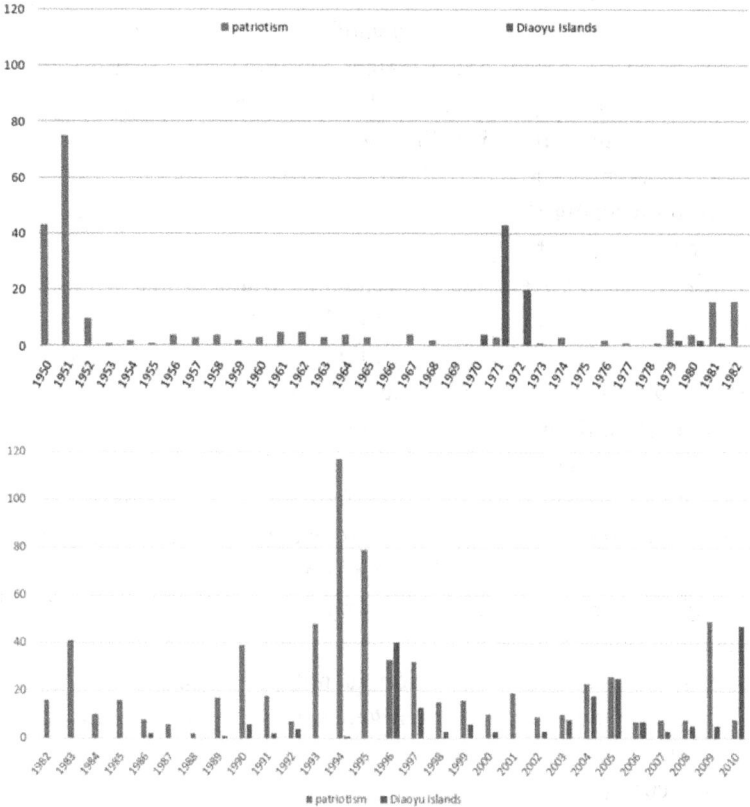

Source: Headline search of "aiguozhuyi" and whole text search of "Diaoyudao" from 1950 to 2010, in DVDs of People's Daily.

However, this modest approach disappeared in 2008, especially after the conclusion of the Beijing Olympic Games. The Chinese navy undertook a number of fleet exercises that crossed into the western Pacific from the East China Sea via waterways along the Ryukyu Islands. The frequency of such exercises grew annually, suggesting they were part of a broader, purposeful strategy. There were only 2 such passages in 2008; by 2013, they had increased sevenfold to 14. These exercises took place in international waters without any violation of international law. They nonetheless triggered concern due to several incidents in which Chinese ship-borne helicopters flew near the Japanese Maritime Self-Defense Force destroyers that were monitoring the vessels.[9] These risky actions could have caused an accident.

The Chinese government has engaged in similar provocative moves with regard to the Senkaku Islands. Beginning in 2008, its ships have encroached on the territorial waters around the Senkakus. The frequency of such incursions gradually rose thereafter, spiking noticeably following the Japanese government's purchase of three of the islands in September 2012. Fifty-two incursions occurred in 2013. This trend indicates that encroachment on the islands' territorial waters also reflects a broader, preplanned initiative.[10] In effect, China is challenging Japan's ownership and control of the islands through physical means, as shown in Figure 2.

China's maritime expansion is not only about the East China Sea. One U.S. naval intelligence officer noted the nature of Chinese goals and actions in a 2013 public forum on maritime security in the following ways:

- "[China's] expansion into the blue waters is largely about countering the U.S. Pacific fleet."

9. Ministry of Defense, *Defense of Japan 2010*, 61, http://www.mod. go.jp/e/publ/w_paper/pdf/2010/ 11Part1_Chapter2_Sec3.pdf.
10. Bonnie S. Glaser, "People's Republic of China Maritime Disputes," statement before the U.S. House Armed Services Subcommittee on Seapower and Projection Forces and the House Foreign Affairs Subcommittee on the Asia Pacific, January 14, 2014, 4, http://csis.org/files/ attachments/ts140114_glaser.pdf.

- "The PLA Navy is going to sea to learn how to do naval warfare.... Make no mistake: the PRC navy is focused on war at sea, and sinking an opposing fleet."

- "If you map out [the] harassments [by the China Marine Surveillance] you will see that they form a curved front that has over time expanded out against the coast of China's neighbours, becoming the infamous nine-dashed line, plus the entire East China Sea...."

- "China is negotiating for control of other nations' resources off their coasts; what's mine is mine, and we'll negotiate what's yours."

- "China Marine Surveillance cutters have no other mission but to harass other nations into submitting to China's expansive claims.... China Marine Surveillance is a full-time maritime sovereignty harassment organisation."

Figure 2. Frequency of Chinese Incursions into the Territorial Waters of the Senkaku Islands, as well as the Frequency of Chinese Naval Vessels Crossing the Ryukyu Islands, 2008–2013[11]

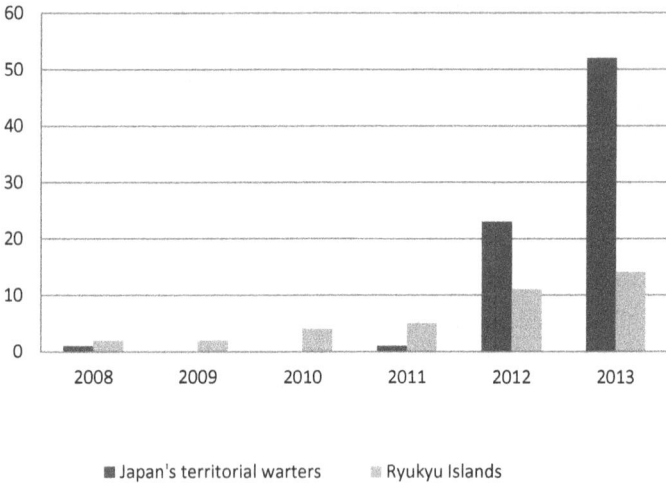

- Japan's territorial warters   Ryukyu Islands

This transformation started in 2008.[12] Apart from the 2008 consensus agreement with Japan for developing resources in the East China Sea, Beijing has not compromised in any outstanding territorial or maritime sovereignty dispute since it resolved its dispute with Russia in 2004.[13]

According to the "rising trend" hypothesis, the incumbent Xi

11. Data from *Defense of Japan (from 2008 to 2013)*, *Yomiuri Shimbun*, *Asahi Shimbun*, *Sankei Shimbun*, *Kyodo News* and *Jiji Press*. "Chugoku Kosento niyoru Senkaku Syoto Shuhen no Setuzokusuiiki nai nyuiki oyobi Ryokai Shinnyu Sekisu (Tsukibetsu)" [Monthly Statistics of Entry of Contiguous Zones and Violation of Territorial Waters of Senkaku Islands by Chinese Government Ships], *Japan Coast Guard*, http://www.kaiho.mlit.go.jp/senkaku/index.html.
12. "Blunt Words on China from US Navy," *Lowy Institute Interpreter*, February 5, 2013, http://www.lowyinterpreter. org/post/2013/02/05/Blunt-words-on-China-from-US-Navy.aspx.
13. Swaine and Fravel, "China's Assertive Behavior, Part Two," 14.

Jinping administration is continuing along this path that began under Hu Jintao in 2008 or 2009. This hypothesis holds that China passed a point of no return in 2009. The hypothesis predicts that the number of incursions will continue to increase. A China with greater economic security and more military power will cease to make compromises and will shed self-imposed behavioral constraints. Given that the underlying conditions for China's assertiveness—its economic and military capacity—are well established, this hypothesis implies that this rising trend will continue, at least in the foreseeable future.

"CYCLE OF DETERIORATION AND AMELIORATION" HYPOTHESIS

The "cycle" hypothesis focuses heavily on the impact of two domestic factors on China's external behavior: the economy and varying approaches to foreign relations by different Chinese leaders. It also presupposes that deterioration of China's external relations is often triggered by the perceived misbehavior of other nations, and that China's negative "overreaction" further worsens the situation. The fact that the Chinese government places such high priority on economic growth compels it to constantly seek better relations with neighbors, which it would not do in the absence of such a rationale. This is one of the reasons that the "rising trend" thesis does not have as much explanatory power as it might appear.

The "cycle" hypothesis holds that 1982 was the critical turning point of Chinese foreign policy. With the launching of the diplomatic strategy of "independent foreign policy of peace" (*dulizizhu de hepingwaijiao*), China began to expend a great deal of effort to achieve amicable relations with its neighbors with economic goals under peaceful circumstances in mind.[14]

---

14. Tomoyuki Kojima, *Gendai Chugoku no Seiji: Sono Riron to Jissen* [Politics of Contemporary China: Theory and Practice] (Tokyo: Keio University Press, 1999), chapter 7.

Even when frictions with partners resulted from disagreements over domestic problems in China, Beijing ensured, time and time again, that relations reverted to the status quo ante.

One instance that illustrates this mechanism is the Tiananmen Square incident. China's relationship with the United States, Europe, and Japan soured after the Chinese government used force to suppress a democratization movement in Tiananmen Square in 1989. However, the Chinese government then worked for several years to mend its relations with these major powers. One concrete example of this attempt was the successful invitation of the Japanese Emperor Hirohito to Beijing in 1992. Japan was the first developed country in the western world to lift economic sanctions against China after the Tiananmen Massacre.

Intraparty differences and power struggles among senior-level members of the CPC also resulted in these alternating periods of "deterioration" and "amelioration." Since the Chinese leadership cadre began to strategically cultivate patriotism among the population in the 1980s, the adverse impact of this "patriotism strategy" upon the Sino-Japanese relationship has concerned many individuals in the Chinese leadership. Yet there is great variation on how leaders handle this matter on a practical level.

For instance, leaders like Hu Yaobang always sought stable ties with Japan, as they perceived Japan to be a key player for China's economic development.[15] By contrast, Jiang Zemin remained highly critical of Japan and did not mind seeing the Sino-Japanese relationship fray.[16] In turn, Hu Jintao, the successor to Jiang, successfully returned bilateral relations with Japan to a state of "normalcy." He, like his faction leader and political mentor Hu Yaobang, understood the poison of na-

15. Yoshikazu Shimizu, *Chugoku wa Naze "Han-Nichi" ni Nattaka* [Why Has China Become "Anti-Japanese"?] (Tokyo: Bungeishunju Ltd., 2003), 117–21.
16. Ibid., chapter 7.

tionalism and believed that Japan was a critical player in the region.[17] Xi Jinping, however, is following in the footsteps of Jiang Zemin on this issue: He places a lower priority on relations with Japan, rather favoring invocations of patriotism-based loyalty for the purpose of preserving political stability within China. On the whole, as factions gain or lose power in China, their rises and falls accentuate the alternating waves of "deterioration" and "amelioration" in China's foreign relations with the world, including in its relationship with Japan.

Unfortunately for Japan, those leaders who believe Japan is important tended to lose the intraparty power struggles. For instance, when Hu Yaobang lost power in 1985, he was accused of maintaining a close relationship with the then-Japanese prime minister, Yasuhiro Nakasone.[18] Moreover, some hypothesize that the anti-Japan protests that repeatedly took place under the reign of Hu Jintao may have been a calculated "backlash" against the pro-Japan faction orchestrated by Jiang Zemin.[19] If this hypothesis holds true, it suggests that tensions between China and Japan over the Senkaku Islands in 2012 may have originated from the intraparty power game during the transition period of leadership from Hu Jintao to Xi Jinping.

To be sure, the leadership aspect of the "cycle" hypothesis is not absolute. Jiang Zemin, for example, was not always critical of Japan; he did seek amelioration occasionally.[20] Similarly, Hu Jintao sometimes took a hardline stance vis-à-vis Japan. For example, Japanese Prime Minister Junichiro Koizumi's annual

---

17. Ibid., chapter 8.
18. Yasuhiro Nakasone, *Tenchi Yujo: Sengo Seiji Gojunen wo Kataru* [Mercy in the Heaven and on Earth: Straight Talk on Fifty-Year Post-War Politics in Japan] (Tokyo: Bungei Shunju Press, 1996), 461–65; Allen S. Whiting, *China Eyes Japan* (Berkeley: University of California Press, 1989), 237–40.
19. Tomoyuki Kojima, *Kukki Suru Chugoku: Nihon wa do Chugoku to Mukiaunoka?* [Rise of China: How Should Japan Deal with China?] (Tokyo: Ashi Shobo, 2005), 32–37.
20. Shimizu, *Chugoku wa Naze "Han-Nichi" ni Nattaka*, chapter 2.

visits to the Yasukuni Shrine, a location perceived as a symbol of militarism by the Chinese, meant that Hu Jintao could not maintain his pro-Japanese policies. Hu made a decision to ameliorate relations with Japan in 2006 simply because Koizumi left office and the new Prime Minister Shinzo Abe implied that he would not to go to the shrine. In general, most leaders attempted to revert back to a state of normalcy in their relations with Japan when relations soured.

One of the most prominent illustrations of this phenomenon was the friction that occurred in China-Japan relations after 2010. Tensions began in September 2010 when a Chinese fishing boat collided with a Japan Coast Guard patrol boat within the territorial waters of the Senkaku Islands. China's attitude stiffened upon learning that the captain of the Chinese fishing boat had been arrested and detained by Japanese authorities. Subsequently, the Chinese government took a combative approach by detaining four Japanese nationals living in China who had no connections with the incident and by imposing a ban on exports of rare earth elements to Japan.[21] Subsequently, China had to change course after its actions triggered a backlash from the international community. Dai Bingguo, a state councilor, published a paper that stressed China's intention to maintain "peaceful development,"[22] and China began to promote a state-directed attempt to improve ties with Japan.

Another example of the cycle of deterioration and amelioration took place after September 2012, when the Japanese government purchased three of the Senkaku Islands. Although China released press comments that were highly critical of Japan, it subsequently sought to mend relations. According to the "cycle" hypothesis, this reversal in China's attitude can be

---

21. Denny Roy, *Return of the Dragon: Rising China and Regional Security* (New York: Colombia University Press, 2013), 93–95.
22. Dai Bingguo, "Jianchi Zou Heping Fazhan Daolu" [We Firmly Take a Route of Peaceful Development], Ecns.cn, December 7, 2010, http://www.chinanews.com/gn/2010/12-07/2704984.shtml.

attributed to the subsiding of the intraparty power struggle that occurred between the 18th National Congress of the Communist Party of November 2012 and the National People's Congress of March 2013, during which a succession struggle for membership in the new Central Politburo (and its standing committee) and the State Council took place. The Chinese government first made a proposal to ameliorate its relations with Japanese officials in March 2013, leading to numerous international exchanges between September and October.[23] These efforts did not culminate in a summit, however. Table 1 shows how these events fit into a "cycle of deterioration and amelioration."

Table 1. Examples of China's Provocation and Attempt to Amend Ties with Japan from September 2012 to November 2013[24]

Period	Provocations	Attempts to amend relations
Sep. 2012	• Violent anti-Japanese demonstrations	
Dec. 2012	• Violation of airspace of Senkaku Islands	

23. "Senkaku, Yuzurenu Ichinen: Dakyoan, Shushogawa ga Isshu" [One Year of No Compromise on Senkaku: PM Abe Rejects China's Proposal of Compromise], *Asahi Shimbun*, September 11, 2013; "Shu Shuseki, Tai-Nichi Kaizen wo Mosaku, Juyo Kaigi de 'Keizai Koryu' Shiji, Tairitsu Jotai Furieki, Chugoku" [President Xi Tries to Seek Amelioration of Relations with Japan: 'Economic Exchanges' Were Directed since Rivalry Is Not Beneficial to China], *Jiji Press*, November 15, 2013, http://www.jiji.com/jc/zc?k=201311/2013111500739&g=pol.
24. The nationality of submarines detected in contiguous zones of the Ryukyu Islands is not formally confirmed by Japanese officials.

Feb. 2013	• Fire control radar lock-on Maritime Self-Defense Force (MSDF) helicopter and vessel	• Xi Jinping's meeting with chief representative of ruling New Komeito, Natsuo Yamaguchi
Mar. 2013		• Proposal to improve relations with Japanese officials
May 2013	• Chinese submarine spotted in waters off of Okinawa	
Aug. 2013		• Reduction of tensions around the Senkaku Islands
Sep. 2013	• First UAV (drone) flight over the East China Sea	• Xi Jinping and Shinzo Abe meet and shake hands at the G-20 meeting • CITIC delegation visits Japan
Oct. 2013		• China sends a secret envoy to Japan • 35th anniversary ceremony of the Sino-Japanese Peace and Friendship Treaty • Xi Jinping makes an accommodative speech on diplomacy toward neighboring nations
Nov. 2013	• Announcement of Air Defense Identification Zone (ADIZ)	

Source: Author's compilation of reports by *Asahi Shimbun*, *Nikkei Shimbun*, *Sankei Shimbun*, and *Jiji Press*.

In short, the "cycle" hypothesis holds that China's current behavior is just a continuation of its omnidirectional foreign policy to achieve continuous economic growth and maintain domestic stability. It suggests that the Chinese government *wants* to revert back to normalcy in its relations with Japan even when frictions occur. An implication is that neighbors can expect such behavior from China in the future. This is because fraying ties with countries like Japan and the Philippines can ultimately result in a strategic confrontation with their most important ally, the United States. As long as China places its economic development and political stability as its highest priorities, China will continue to make efforts to ameliorate relations with neighbors. The hypothesis shows that there are limits to China's hardline approach.

"REDEFINITION OF STRATEGIC RIVALS" HYPOTHESIS
The third hypothesis is "redefinition of strategic rivals." Some of China's strategic goals or discourse to describe China's stance on external issues are quite distant from current realities. For example, China insists that China is not divided, that Taiwan is a part of China, and that most of the East and South China Seas are under China's sovereignty. China has confronted its neighbors and strategic rivals in order to narrow the gap between its goals and reality.

This hypothesis supposes that China is always in conflict with some of its neighbors and at least one strategic rival because of the balance this strikes in its strategic relations. For instance, before the Sino-Soviet split, China's major strategic rival was the United States. Thereafter, however, the United States and China moved more closely together as a bulwark to Soviet power. Such maneuvering can be seen in China's relations today. Thus, the behavioral patterns of Chinese diplomacy have not fundamentally changed; what has changed since the 1950s is which country China confronts and the intensity of that confrontation.

Table 2 makes clear that the People's Republic of China and the Communist Party of China have never achieved friendly relationships with all their neighbors or other strategically significant countries. For example, following the Communist Party's victory in the Chinese Civil War, it kept confronting the Kuomintang in Taiwan militarily; there has yet to be an end to the confrontation in the Taiwan Strait.

Taiwan and the United States have played the role of major Chinese "rivals" since the Korean War (for relations with the United States, the period of Sino-Soviet enmity is an exception). For the Chinese government, the image of the United States has shifted from direct to indirect rival since normalization. This gave China the impetus to redefine constantly its relations with the United States by bringing up new strategic concepts like "strategic partnership" and a "new type of major-power relationship."

Table 2. Direct and Indirect Rivals of the People's Republic of China/Communist Party of China

Content	Period	Direct rivals	Indirect rivals
Civil War through Sino-U.S. normalization	1946– 1972/1978	Kuomintang/ Taiwan	U.S.
Korean War through Sino-U.S. normalization	1950– 1972/1978	U.S., Republic of Korea	
Indo-China conflict (including Vietnam War and civil war in Cambodia)	1950–1991		France, U.S., USSR
Sino-Soviet confrontation	1960–1989	USSR, Mongolia	

Sino-Indian border conflict	1962	India	USSR
Sino-Vietnamese war	1979	Vietnam	USSR
Third Taiwan Strait crisis through Chen Shui-bian	1995–2008	Taiwan	U.S.
China's assertive engagement with South China Sea	1974–present	Vietnam, Philippines	U.S.
China's assertive engagement with Senkaku Islands	2008–present	Japan	U.S.

Source: Author's compilation.

If the underlying assumptions of the "redefinition" hypothesis are correct, it is possible to make the following inferences. As compared to the 1950s, China is expected to be more conciliatory in its diplomacy. A quick review of diplomatic history is of use here. In the 1950s, China fought the United States in the Korean War. Thereafter, it had a confrontational relationship with Taiwan for a long period of time. China had also fought India, Vietnam, and the Soviet Union. The Chinese government shifted gears dramatically in the 1980s, when its diplomatic approach was not based on a (hypothetical) "major enemy" and it gave top priority to economic development. China actively *avoided* creating enmity or a potential for military confrontation with other countries. The fact that since 1979 the Chinese government adopted a peaceful unification policy and therefore did not order the PLA to attack Taiwan supports this contention. More recently, during frictions over the Senkaku Islands with Japan, China was careful not to provoke military engagement. In short, there is a clear trend of declining behavioral hawkishness, which is incompatible with the "rising trend" hypothesis from the long-term perspective.

Other examples are also illustrative. For one, when Sino-Soviet ties were at their nadir, China hedged by eagerly improving relations with the United States. Thereafter, when the Sino-Soviet split subsided, there was less of a threat to China from overland aggression. This led China to be confrontational toward Taiwan and its ultimate guarantor, the United States. Another example occurred in 2008, during the executive transition from the Democratic Progressive Party (DPP) to the Kuomintang (KMT). As a result, the Chinese and Taiwanese governments drew closer quickly, which gave China the "strategic space" to adopt a more hawkish attitude toward politics over the South China Sea and the East China Sea. In truth, China grew more hostile to Japan and the Philippines. In short, if the "redefinition" hypothesis is correct, it predicts that China selectively confronts rivals to secure its interests while avoiding being strategically surrounded by hostile neighbors and major powers at the same time.

Moreover, the "redefinition" thesis also predicts that confrontation depends not only on China's own strategic choices but also on its neighbors' diplomatic troubles. This is because Chinese strategic interests range from territorial ambitions to rivalries over rights at sea. Put differently, history has shown that China is a "patient" actor. Its hawkishness occurs immediately after some potential adversary commits a diplomatic mistake. Well-prepared hawks remain in decisionmaking positions, taking advantage of their adversary's mistake. As mentioned earlier, the International Crisis Group contends that China's actions reflect a "reactively assertive" tactic, often used in the South China Sea, whereby it exploits perceived provocations by other countries in disputed areas to change the status quo in its favor.[25]

The "redefinition" hypothesis predicts that China may grow more conciliatory toward Japan and the Philippines if a hos-

25. International Crisis Group, "Dangerous Waters," 12–15.

tile leader comes to power in neighboring countries like India, Taiwan, or the United States. In addition, when Japan and the Philippines have pro-China leaders, China might make minimal compromises for amelioration of tensions.

Finally, despite changes for the better in specific bilateral alliances, this hypothesis predicts that an assertive China will continue and always be present in certain issues in the future as long as its strategic ambitions are not completely satisfied.

POLICY IMPLICATIONS

The three hypotheses explained above offer distinct policy implications for China's neighbors and for the United States.

The first policy implication draws on the "rising trend" hypothesis. If this hypothesis is correct, a strategy of hedging will be desirable for China's neighbors and the United States. Hedging requires these neighbors to be more cooperative with each other to face Chinese power. China will inevitably have tensions with neighbors such as Japan, the Philippines, Taiwan, and Vietnam, whose geographical location "blocks" the expansion of Chinese strategic influence. These neighbors, on the other hand, will resist China's simultaneous expansion of economic and military power, and concomitant assertive foreign policy behavior, as Edward Luttwak argues.[26]

In this scenario, friction does not necessarily emanate from deteriorating relations between China and another neighbor but from the dynamics of the period of power transition. In other words, friction is a symptom rather than a cause. China's neighbors will have to turn to the United States as the regional but geographically remote balancer to minimize friction. At the same time, as a regional great power Japan will be expected to take a greater role in this transition period. One example is

26. Luttwak, *The Rise of China vs. the Logic of Strategy*, chapter 11.

that the Philippines seeks greater cooperation not only with the United States but also with Japan.[27]

As for the United States, its options are limited to accepting the call for greater engagement in East Asia. The reasoning is straightforward: For China, the United States is a "strategic competitor" and China seeks to dominate the United States' allies and security partners. Greater engagement, however, may invite hedging against the United States by China, which is likely to result in a vicious cycle in East Asia. To minimize this possibility, China's neighbors have an incentive both to seek greater cooperation with the United States and to strengthen engagement with China.

The second policy implication rests on the "cycle of deterioration and amelioration" hypothesis. If this hypothesis is correct, neighboring governments will prioritize strengthening engagement diplomacy vis-à-vis China in recognition that overall China's development is built on a peaceful and stable strategic environment. Moreover, this hypothesis implies that China *will* ameliorate its relations with its neighbors after relations sour. Put differently, it is reasonable for other nations to expect that doves will eventually return to leading positions in decisionmaking even when hawks appear to be predominant in setting China's strategic course; previously this has occurred in economic relations.

In this scenario, China's neighbors like Japan and the Philippines have an opportunity to improve ties with China. They may adopt a strategy of patience and seek to keep engaging China until doves return to leading positions in China. They have to avoid "provocative" words and actions in order to maintain good political atmosphere with China. However, it

---

27. "Kaijo Keibi Kyoka de Junshitei 10 Seki wo Kyoyo: Nichi-Hi Shuno-kaidan" [Japan Supplies 10 Patrol Boats to the Philippines for Enhancing Maritime Security: Japan-Philippine Summit Meeting], *Nikkei Shimbun*, July 27, 2013.

is important to bear in mind that once China's relationship with another country becomes tense, it puts strong political and psychological pressures on it by preserving its position and even by resorting to coercive means. China also engages in negative campaigns to undermine the diplomatic image of its adversary. Such tactics will strengthen the influence of the conservatives and hawks in the target nation, making it more difficult to reach a compromise. For the target nation to minimize this possibility and improve relations with China (even reluctantly through compromise), it will be critical to keep hawks marginalized in the domestic political debate.

In addition, the governments of China's neighbors now in conflict with China should examine why other states succeeded in improving relations with China. For instance, Russia has reached a strategic partnership agreement with China, which provides arms sought by China. The two countries are unlikely to revert to a frictional relationship because they have addressed territorial disputes through negotiation. Another example is Taiwan, which has also improved its ties with mainland China. Since 2008, the Taiwanese authorities have offered a "compromise" deal by officially invoking the "1992 consensus" that included "one China." Countries like Japan and the Philippines could study these cases to see if relevant diplomatic lessons can be applied to their ties with China.

The third and final policy implication builds on the "redefinition of strategic rivals" hypothesis. If this hypothesis is correct, China's neighboring governments should ensure constantly that they avoid being targeted by China's enmity. It is critical to note that any neighbor can be a "rival" of China. This hypothesis also suggests that when China ends friction with one country, it directs enmity to another. At the same time, this hypothesis suggests that the United States should reevaluate its alliance strategy and take a more regional approach by not reacting separately to each event involving a specific ally or security partner.

Today's Sino-Japanese frictions may capture this dynamic. The Chinese government is putting pressure on Japanese Prime Minister Abe, which used to be directed at former Taiwanese leaders such as Lee Teng-hui and Chen Shui-bian. At the same time, China sought to win cooperation from the United States by framing the Taiwanese leadership as the trouble maker.[28] This label has been transferred to Japan. In this way, China seeks to drive wedges between the United States and its allies because it understands American reluctance to be involved in frictions with China through its allies' and security partners' "trivial matters."

In this scenario, it is Asian nations that are more likely than China to be compelled to make compromises when diplomatic friction between those countries and China escalates. This is because the United States always finds it easier to ask its friends and allies to be more conciliatory than to ask China. At the same time, however, no sovereign state wants to compromise its territory or political independence. This leads to a diplomatic impasse and also invites dissatisfaction or criticism from the United States. Pressure from China targets precisely this point.

As a consequence, the third hypothesis suggests that the countries and governments that are targeted by China must escape this vicious cycle. This is not impossible, as the case of Taiwan demonstrates. Thus, if Japan offers "empty compromises" to China over the sovereignty of the Senkaku Islands through carefully designed diplomatic wording, it can improve its relations with China, albeit temporarily. Yet it remains to be seen if this would lead Japan out of the vicious cycle and into

---

28. Yasuhiro Matsuda, "Taiwan's Partisan Politics and Its Impact on U.S.-Taiwanese Relations," *Journal of Social Science* 63, no. 3/4 (December 2011): 73–94, http://jww.iss.u-tokyo.ac.jp/jss/pdf/jss630304_073094.pdf.

a virtuous cycle. Moreover, such a move would have spillover effects on other Asian nations like the Philippines, Taiwan, and Vietnam if a regional great power such as Japan has to submit to China on critical issues such as territorial sovereignty under paramilitary pressure. In this case, the strategic power balance in East Asia will tilt—perhaps irrevocably—toward China. Another implication of this dynamic is that countries with poor relations with China should engage other regional powers. This is because, as explained previously, China's redefinition of its strategic rivals accounts for the status of its relations with states other than that rival, including possible "swing states" such as the Republic of Korea (ROK) or countries like Cambodia in Southeast Asia. China's maintenance of healthy ties is driven partially by its need to focus its energies on dealing with strategic rivals such as the United States and Japan. If the latter nations can improve their relationships with the ROK and some Southeast Asian countries, this will compel China to adjust its policies both because it will have to increase its efforts in those neighbors to maintain influence and because better ties with targeted nations may cause swing states to be less supportive of China's position towards targeted nations.

CONCLUSION: CHALLENGES TO CHINA'S NEIGHBORS AND THE UNITED STATES

The three hypotheses examined in this paper each have their own merits, despite the shortcomings in explanatory power mentioned previously. Each captures some dimension of "truth" in Asia's strategic relations. It can even be assumed that each hypothesis *is* accurate, or that the three of them are correlated, if one believes in the spiral-like evolution of history. If so, one can make the following prediction: that China's hawkish assertiveness will escalate as its national power expands and that China will direct enmity to a specific country or group to isolate it or them. But once the strategic situation is seen as turning or in actuality turns against it, China will seek some solution by attempting to improve relations with the target nation at the most propitious moment. This brings all three hypotheses into play when explaining China's relations.

Most of the nations that have experienced diplomatic conflicts or impasses with China following the end of the Cold War are allies or security partners of the United States. Their political status in Asia reflects the regional order constructed by the United States after World War II and during the Cold War. Today, this balance is in flux as power tilts toward China. Regardless of the predictive power of the three hypotheses, the United States might at times view its allies and security partners as "trouble makers"—no matter how hard these governments work to keep close ties with the United States—because they risk bringing the United States into conflict with China, so long as China avoids direct confrontation with the United States.

As William Blake once said, "It is easier to forgive an enemy than to forgive a friend." This quote is ever more meaningful in contemporary strategic conditions in East Asia, because expectations for strategic friends and those for strategic adversaries are completely different. Humans expect more from friends than from rivals: they expect friends to fully support them. They do not expect much from rivals—absence of friction is enough. Close friends and family members clash with each other precisely because expectations of support are high. People might lose friends as a result. When this happens, how will the rival react? Will it become friendly or even more hostile?

Looking toward the future, it is important to consider that the spiral of Chinese relations with other nations may look different when China has more power. Maybe the cycles will be smaller, or China will have more sticks and fewer carrots, or bigger sticks and bigger carrots. Or the calculation of strategic rivalry will be different because correlation of other forces won't scare China as much. Ultimately, if China's GDP surpasses that of the United States and all the Chinese neighbors submit to it, will the United States be defined as a direct rival or will China's strategic rivalries finally end?

China's diplomatic inflexibility and determined behavior pose major challenges not just to its neighbors but also to the United States. The United States should have a grand strategy to address this challenge. Thus far, the U.S. "rebalance" to Asia is more like a slogan than a concrete strategic plan. U.S. policies toward friends and allies surrounding China should be components of the larger strategy, not an accumulation of sporadic reactions. U.S. allies and security partners also should integrate themselves into this strategy through frequent strategic dialogues and consultations with the United States. ∎

3. U.S.-JAPAN ALLIED MARITIME STRATEGY: BALANCING THE RISE OF MARITIME CHINA

Tetsuo Kotani

China's growing maritime power is changing the strategic balance among Asian powers. The continental power of Russia, China, and India dominates the Asian landmass, while the maritime power of the United States and Japan secures freedom of the seas in the western Pacific. Neither side has traditionally been able to project substantial conventional power into the realm of the other.[1] Now, however, the development of China's anti-access/area denial (A2/AD) capabilities is challenging U.S.-Japan maritime supremacy in the Asian littoral.

China has become more assertive, intensifying its territorial and maritime claims in the East and South China Seas. The announcement of China's air defense identification zone (ADIZ) in the East China Sea and the harassment of the USS *Cowpens* in the South China Sea are just recent examples of Beijing's attempts to deny access by other maritime powers to its Near Seas (the Yellow Sea and the East and South China Seas), which are enclosed by the first island chain (a chain of islands from Kyushu, Okinawa, to Taiwan and Borneo). The first sec-

---

1. Michael McDevitt, "The Evolving Maritime Security Environment in East Asia: Implications for the US-Japan Alliance," *PacNet*, no. 33, May 31, 2012.

tion of this paper analyzes the implications of China's A2/AD strategy through the two traditional naval concepts of *fortress fleet* and *fleet-in-being*.

The United States has made clear its intention to rebalance toward the Asia-Pacific, recognizing the challenges and opportunities posed by the rise of Asia as a whole and China in particular. It is not that the United States is "returning" to Asia; it never left this dynamic region. The rebalance requires the United States to maintain sustainable forces and power-projection capability to counter A2/AD threats in the region.[2] The second section provides an overview of the U.S. rebalance policy and options for a new U.S. maritime strategy.

Japan, under Prime Minister Shinzo Abe, has just adopted the first National Security Strategy (NSS) for "proactive contribution to peace." Abe is also upgrading Japan's security policy through the establishment of a National Security Council (NSC) and the revision of the National Defense Program Guidelines (NDPG). Tokyo now aims to balance the rise of China through strategic diplomacy and to reinforce deterrence toward China by setting up a "dynamic joint defense force" to defend the Nansei Islands in the southwest of the Japanese archipelago. The third section of this paper reviews the implications and challenges of the strategic diplomacy and "dynamic joint defense force" concepts.

Finally, as Tokyo and Washington have agreed to revise their bilateral defense guidelines by the end of 2014, this paper provides some recommendations for this revision.

UNDERSTANDING CHINA'S A2/AD STRATEGY

China's A2/AD strategy can be understood better through two traditional naval concepts: fortress fleet and fleet-in-being.[3]

---

2. U.S. Department of Defense, *Sustaining U.S. Global Leadership: Priorities for 21st Century Defense* (Washington, DC: U.S. Department of Defense, January 2012).

3. Christian Le Mière explains China's maritime strategy with the

The fortress-fleet concept, as the American historian and naval strategist Alfred Thayer Mahan described and criticized, refers to a fleet that operates under cover of shore-based fire support as part of static coastal defenses. The concept of fleet-in-being—introduced by the British Adm. Arthur Herbert, Earl of Torrington in the 17th century—describes actions by an inferior fleet to undermine a stronger fleet through limited offensives or merely the very existence of the fleet.

China's Fortress Fleet

Mahan observed the performance of the Russian Navy in the Russo-Japanese War of 1904–05 as defensive, both strategically and tactically. Russian admirals kept their main fleet passively in port to defend coastal land features while sheltering the fleet under the fort's big guns. Mahan criticized the Russians' defensive strategic mentality for limiting the fleet's freedom to maneuver and for avoiding any battle that might have advanced their strategic goals.[4] Russia did not have a monopoly on this defensive mindset; the strategy was applied by other continental powers, including the People's Republic of China.[5]

For China, using coastal defense to deny seaborne invasion is a historical requirement. China, despite its 8,700-mile coastline and great navigable rivers running to the Pacific, long remained a self-sufficient land power, facing the constant pressure of armed nomads across land borders. Its century of humiliation started in the mid-19th century, when Western

"fleet-in-being" concept in Le Mière, "America's Pivot to East Asia: The Naval Dimension," *Survival* 54 no. 3 (June–July 2012): 81–94; James R. Holmes explains with the concept of "fortress fleet" in Holmes, "A 'Fortress Fleet' for China," *Whitehead Journal of Diplomacy and International Relations* (Summer/Fall 2010): 115–28.

4. Holmes, "A 'Fortress Fleet' for China," 117.

5. Clark G. Reynolds, *Navies in History* (Annapolis, MD: Naval Institute Press, 1998), 62.

powers exploited China's vulnerable maritime approaches. China's strategic weakness comes from the sea.

The concept of a fortress fleet thus fits China's history. The missions of a continental power's navy are subordinate to those of its army.[6] Accordingly, the People's Liberation Army Navy (PLA Navy, or PLAN) assumes a defensive strategic posture. The PLAN augments the army's coastal fortifications to help repel amphibious invasions. It also supports the PLA so that the army can take the offensive on the continent where China enjoys vast strategic depth, complex terrain, and massive manpower reserves. In short, the PLAN has been a fortress fleet by nature.

Adm. Liu Huaqing, the "father" of the PLAN, changed China's maritime doctrine in the 1980s. Liu envisioned better coastal defense by expanding the PLAN's operational areas out to the first and second island chains.[7] In recent years, advances in military technologies have changed the implications for the modern fortress fleet. Land-based aircraft carrying antiship cruise missiles have greatly expanded the reach and accuracy of coastal defenses, providing bold access-denial capabilities to strike U.S. expeditionary groups hundreds of miles away from the Chinese coast. Plus, antiship weapons are cheaper than aircraft carriers. These relatively inexpensive weapons can keep the formidable U.S. sea-control fleet further offshore.[8]

China is adding a shore-based carrier killer to its A2/AD arsenal. It has been developing and testing this antiship ballistic missile (ASBM), based on the DF-21 medium-range ballistic missile, which could target moving U.S. aircraft carriers. Huge technological challenges remain, but mastering such a technology would be a "game-changer" in today's strategic cal-

---

6. Ibid., 4.
7. Andrew Scobell and Andrew J. Nathan, "China's Overstretched Military," *Washington Quarterly* 35, no. 4 (Fall 2012).
8. Holmes, "A 'Fortress Fleet' for China," 118.

culus. A successful ASBM program would greatly restrict the offensive strike capabilities of U.S. carrier strike groups in the western Pacific and undermine the credibility of U.S. defense commitments in Asia.

An important development for the fortress fleet of the 21st century is that high technology allows the fleet to leave the port. The concept of a fortress fleet originally referred to strategic and tactical defensive, when shore-based fire support reached only several miles. Today's fortress fleet can be offensive, at least in tactical operations, under the aegis of longer-range antiship missiles and submarines. As a result, the PLAN has become more assertive in the Asian littoral.

Chinese Fleet-in-Being

Admiral Arthur Herbert, Earl of Torrington, decided not to engage the superior French fleet in the War of the League of Augsburg in 1690. The French were threatening to invade England but Torrington was confident that as long as he had a fleet-in-being they would not make the attempt. He favored keeping his fleet at the mouth of the River Thames and avoided any decisive naval battle until anticipated reinforcements arrived. On the other hand, Torrington employed aggressive tactical offensives to weaken his opponent whenever an opportunity arose.[9] The concept of fleet-in-being assumes temporary strategic defense combined with offensive tactical operations. Once fully reinforced, the fleet can resume the strategic counteroffensive.

The fleet-in-being is a natural consequence of Communist China's strategic tradition. Mao Zedong's Red Army favored aggressive operational tactics, or "active defense," before making a strategic counteroffensive, as seen in the Long March, the Sino-Japanese War of the 1930s–40s, and the Chinese Civil War. Likewise, the PLAN's "offshore active defense" concept aims to create conditions for a strategic counteroffensive

---

9. Reynolds, *Navies in History*, 62.

through "people's war at sea," or "guerrilla warfare at sea."[10]

In essence, the fleet-in-being is a sea-denial strategy. The fleet does not seek sea control but attempts to deny enemy control of certain maritime areas through its presence and menace. China's massive submarine fleet and antiship weaponry are its primary tools for sea denial. A2/AD relies on wide-range ocean surveillance to detect and locate approaching enemy forces.[11] As a result, the PLAN encounters other navies more frequently in the Near Seas. In October 2006, for example, a Chinese *Song*-class attack submarine quietly surfaced within nine miles of the aircraft carrier USS *Kitty Hawk* as the forward-deployed flattop sailed on a training exercise in the East China Sea.

On the other hand, the PLAN needs to deny other countries' surveillance activities in the Near Seas. Beijing thus persists in a series of excessive maritime claims—or legal warfare—as a sea denial strategy. China's domestic law guarantees freedom of navigation in its exclusive economic zone (EEZ) but denies such freedom in its "historic waters." Its EEZ claims are based on the historical "occupation" of the waters in the Yellow Sea, East China Sea, and South China Sea.[12] Thus China does not accept surveillance activities by foreign military vessels in its EEZ and fails to recognize the airspace above its EEZ as international airspace. This forms the background to Chinese aggressiveness in the Hainan EP-3 incident in 2001, the USNS *Impeccable* incident in 2009, and the USS *Cowpens* incident in 2013. The announcement of China's ADIZ in the East China Sea is another attempt to deny Japanese and American aerial surveillance.[13]

---

10. Holmes, "A 'Fortress Fleet' for China," 120.
11. McDevitt, "The Evolving Maritime Security Environment in East Asia."
12. James Kraska, *Maritime Power and the Law of the Sea: Expeditionary Operations in World Politics* (New York: Oxford University Press, 2011), 315–6.
13. To understand China's ADIZ, see Peter A. Dutton, "Caelum Liberam: Air Defense Identification Zones outside Sovereign Airspace," *American Journal of International Law* 103 (2009).

China's paramilitary maritime law enforcement ships are also active in the Asian littoral waters.[14] China is now integrating four of the so-called "Five Dragons" into a new Chinese Coast Guard. Those paramilitary ships have been employed in numerous cases, including the harassment of the USNS *Impeccable* near Hainan Island in March 2009, the standoff over the Scarborough Shoal in the Philippine EEZ from April to June 2012, and the confrontation over the Senkaku Islands after September 2012. China has found those paramilitary ships an effective way to demonstrate maritime jurisdiction while challenging other states' claims in contested waters without sending warships.

Despite its carrier and amphibious ship building programs, the PLAN will continue to be weaker than the sea-control fleet of the U.S. Navy in the western Pacific. Hence the fleet-in-being concept makes sense for the PLAN to deter any U.S. intervention. In other words, the PLAN will remain strategically defensive while tactically offensive. On the other hand, China's tactical offensive, especially by paramilitary ships, raises the chance of accidents and unintended escalation.

Implications of China's A2/AD Strategy

The PLAN is a hybrid of fortress fleet and fleet-in-being.[15] The concept of fortress fleet refers to anti-access and the concept of fleet-in-being leads to area denial. Both concepts indicate that the PLAN will become more assertive at the tactical level

14. For an overview of China's maritime law enforcement agencies, see Lyle J. Goldstein, *Five Dragons Stirring Up the Sea: Challenge and Opportunity in China's Improving Maritime Enforcement Capabilities*, China Maritime Study, No. 5 (Newport, RI: U.S. Naval War College, April 2010), http://www.usnwc.edu/Research---Gaming/ China-Maritime-Studies-Institute/ Publications/documents/CMSI_No5_web1.pdf; and International Crisis Group, "Stirring Up the South China Sea," Asia Report No. 223, April 23, 2012, http://www.crisisgroup.org/~/media/Files/asia/northeast-asia/ 223-stirring-up-the-south-china-sea-i.pdf.
15. Holmes, "A 'Fortress Fleet' for China," 124–25.

because of the Red Army's legacy and new affordable advanced technologies. Both concepts also suggest that the PLAN remain strategically defensive. A2/AD is an American term; Chinese strategic thinkers refer to it as "counter-intervention."[16] Thus, in essence, China's maritime strategy is defensive.

An open question remains: In what circumstances would the PLAN launch a strategic counteroffensive? It is unlikely that the PLAN will become a dominant navy in the western Pacific in the foreseeable future. The PLAN needs to remain strategically defensive, at least against the United States. President Xi Jinping's proposal of a "new model of major power relations" indicates that China is seeking a strategic accommodation between China and the United States, or peaceful coexistence, based on "mutual respect for core interests." In other words, China's priority is to force the United States to acknowledge its territorial and maritime claims in the East and South China Seas.

China is seeking strategic stability vis-à-vis the United States. China is the only nuclear weapon-state under the Nuclear Proliferation Treaty (NPT) that is expanding its nuclear arsenal. The lack of a credible sea-based deterrent prevents Beijing from possessing assured destruction capabilities. China is acquiring credible second-strike capabilities with the anticipated introduction of JL-2 SLBMs coupled with DF-31 and DF-41 road-mobile intercontinental ballistic missiles (ICBMs). China also plans to introduce up to five Type 094, or *Jin*-class, strategic nuclear ballistic missile submarines (SSBNs) armed with JL-2 missiles, while constructing an underwater submarine base on Hainan Island in the South China Sea.[17] In addition, China is developing a new hypersonic glide vehicle, which

---

16. McDevitt, "The Evolving Maritime Security Environment in East Asia."

17. Tetsuo Kotani, "Why China Wants the South China Sea," *Diplomat*, July 18, 2011, http://thediplomat.com/2011/07/18/ why-china-wants-the-south-china-sea/.

might add greater strategic strike capability.[18] China might not achieve strategic parity with the United States but it could establish strategic stability with limited deterrence capabilities.

China's search for strategic stability with the United States raises the question of the stability-instability paradox. As China becomes more confident in its deterrent capability that can withstand a U.S. preemptive strike, the PLAN might launch further offensives in the "near seas" to change the territorial status quo.[19] China's neighbors perceive Chinese assertiveness in the Asian littoral as a common threat, and those countries seek stronger ties with the United States. Therefore China attempts to decouple the United States and its allies and friends in Asia by using economic leverage to prevent what it perceives as containment. If the decoupling succeeds, China might not refrain from challenging the existing regional order to legitimate its territorial and maritime claims.

THE U.S. REBALANCE AND ITS IMPLICATIONS

The United States was destined to become a Pacific nation with strong commercial interests in Asia. The United States has maintained forward military presence and unimpeded access to the region in order to overcome the "tyranny of distance." The "Open Door" policy, the San Francisco system, and the Nixon Doctrine all reflected U.S. interests in Asia. To protect its interests, the United States fought a bloody war with Japan and a cold war with the Soviet Union in Asia. Today the rise of China poses both opportunities and challenges for U.S. engage-

---

18. Bill Gertz, "China Conducts First Test of New Ultra-High Speed Missile Vehicle," *Washington Free Beacon*, January 13, 2014, http://free-beacon.com/national-security/china-conducts-first-test-of-new-ultra-high-speed-missile-vehicle/.

19. Brad Roberts, "Extended Deterrence and Strategic Stability in Northeast Asia," National Institute for Defense Studies Japan, Visiting Scholar Paper Series, no. 1, August 9, 2013, http://www.nids.go.jp/english/publication/ visiting/pdf/01.pdf.

ment with Asia. The Obama administration's pivot or rebalance to Asia reflects historical requirements. But the rebalance needs to be backed up by an appropriate military strategy to address A2/AD threats.

The U.S. Sea-Control Fleet and Marines-in-Dispersal

The rebalance requires the United States to reinforce its sea-control fleet in the Pacific. Accordingly, the Pentagon plans to deploy up to four new littoral combat ships (LCSs) to Singapore and the U.S. Navy will assign 60 percent of its entire fleet to the Pacific by 2020. The new naval posture in Asia will strengthen U.S. engagement in the region through calls at regional ports, and engagement with regional navies through activities such as exercises and exchanges. The U.S. Navy is also replacing forward-deployed naval forces in the western Pacific with more capable ships and aircraft and seeking a basing option in Australia.

The U.S. Marines—another important element of U.S. sea power—are dispersing. The U.S. Marine Corps (USMC) now envisions itself as a "middle-weight" force, emphasizing the dispersion of lighter forward-deployed units for rapid response and increased engagement with regional partners for training and capacity building.[20] Since the number of U.S. amphibious ships is insufficient, the Marines seek opportunities to work with the Navy's other platforms. In accordance with the new USMC force structure review, the deployment of up to 2,500 U.S. Marines in Darwin, Australia, was announced in November 2011. In February 2012, it was agreed that 4,700 U.S. Marines in Okinawa would be transferred to Guam, while another 3,300 will be deployed to Hawaii and Australia on a rotational basis.

20. Force Structure Review Committee, *Reshaping America's Expeditionary Force in Readiness: Report of the 2010 Marine Corps* (Washington, DC: Department of the Navy, March 2011), http://community.marines.mil/ community/ Documents/MarineCorpsConnection/e-mail%203-18-11/ forcestructurereview.pdf.

The U.S. rebalance results in a force shift within Asia rather than a shift from the Middle East to Asia. The U.S. military posture in Asia long focused on Northeast Asia, specifically the Korean Peninsula and the Taiwan Strait. To balance the rise of China, however, the United States is shifting its focus from Northeast Asia to the entire Asia-Pacific. The United States is thus seeking opportunities to access the ports of U.S. allies (Australia, the Philippines, and Thailand) and new friends such as Vietnam.

Christian Le Mière described the recent U.S. move as "fleet-in-dispersal" to avoid direct confrontation with China, while hedging against Chinese aggression.[21] Le Mière warns that this strategy would further encourage China's assertiveness due to reduced U.S. presence in China's Near Seas.[22] But the U.S. Navy is increasing the number of ships it deploys in the region and is keeping the sea-control fleet in China's Near Seas, as demonstrated by exercises with Japan in the East China Sea, with South Korea in the Yellow Sea, and with Southeast Asian countries in the South China Sea.

It would be more appropriate to describe the change in the U.S. force structure in Asia as marines-in-dispersal. The reduction of numbers of U.S. Marines in Okinawa and the first island chain does not necessarily encourage China's assertiveness since the 31st Marine Expeditionary Unit (MEU), the first responder to crisis, remains based in Okinawa. In fact, marines-in-dispersal could further contribute to deterrence as long as the strategic mobility of the "middle-weight" Marines is guaranteed. Marines-in-dispersal also ensures increased engagement with regional partners.

The presumption of the U.S. rebalance is stability in other parts of the world. Although the Obama administration has sought to end the wars in Afghanistan and Iraq, the Middle East presents numerous challenges. In particular, the civil war in

21. Le Mière, "America's Pivot to East Asia," 86.
22. Ibid., 92.

Syria and the nuclear program of Iran remain sources of instability. More recently, Russian military intervention in Ukraine
is destabilizing Eastern Europe. If the situation in other parts
of the world becomes worse, the United States would need to
review the rebalance to the Asia-Pacific.

Fiscal constraint is another challenge, and this is one of the
primary issues the 2014 Quadrennial Defense Review (QDR)
addresses. President Obama canceled his trip to Southeast Asia
in October 2013 due to fiscal problems that led to the government shutdown, and regional countries remain concerned
about the feasibility of the rebalance. If the United States fails
to allocate sufficient defense assets to the Asia-Pacific to overcome A2/AD threats, that would undermine the foundation of
the rebalance and the credibility of U.S. commitments to Asia.

In short, there are widespread concerns in the region about
U.S. commitment to the rebalance. Regional countries are not
assured by the U.S. engagement with China. For example, National Security Advisor Susan Rice referred to the operational-
ization of a "new model of major power relations" in her speech
on the rebalance.[23] Such a statement would just encourage
China to seek further accommodations from the United States.
U.S. defense leaders also emphasize their willingness to expand
mil-to-mil ties between the United States and China. Engagement with China is necessary, but the Obama administration
should reassure allies and friends at the same time.

Air-Sea Battle or Offshore Control?
China is expanding its A2/AD capabilities. But the United States
does not accept a situation that would deny the U.S. access to
the western Pacific. This is not an arms race, as seen in the early
20th century, when a naval buildup program occupied a large

23. Susan E. Rice, "America's Future in Asia" (remarks as prepared
for delivery at Georgetown University, Washington, DC, November
20, 2013), http://www.whitehouse.gov/the-press-office/2013/11/21/
remarks-prepared- delivery-national-security-advisor-susan-e-rice.

part of the national budget. Instead, the region is witnessing a "military capabilities competition" between assured access and access denial.[24]

The United States has been developing the concept of Air-Sea Battle (ASB) to maintain freedom of action under A2/AD threats.[25] ASB is not a strategy but a tactical concept designed to attack-in-depth through integrated operations across five domains (air, land, sea, space, and cyberspace). It preserves the ability to defeat aggression and maintain escalation dominance despite the challenges posed by advanced A2/AD threats. Its central idea is to develop networked, integrated forces capable of attack-in-depth to disrupt, destroy, and defeat adversary forces (NIA/D3). NIA/D3 requires three basic actions: (1) disrupt enemy surveillance systems (command, control, communications, computers, intelligence, surveillance, and reconnaissance or C4ISR); (2) destroy enemy precision weapon launching systems; and (3) defeat enemy missiles and other weapons.

ASB has caused widespread controversy among U.S. strategic thinkers.[26] ASB addresses the maintenance of power projection under A2/AD threats to deter potential aggressors while reassuring U.S. allies and partners by demonstrating U.S. determination. ASB provides a wide range of striking options, and the promoters of ASB have emphasized the importance of striking military assets on Chinese territory. But critics raise concerns about its escalatory nature. ASB assumes penetra-

24. McDevitt, "The Evolving Maritime Security Environment in East Asia."

25. The details of the Air-Sea Battle are classified, but its essence is now available at U.S. Department of Defense, "Air-Sea Battle," May 2013, http://www.defense.gov/pubs/ASB-ConceptImplementation-Summary-May-2013.pdf.

26. For example, see Elbridge Colby, "Don't Sweat AirSea Battle," *National Interest*, July 31, 2013, http://nationalinterest.org/commentary/dont-sweat-airsea-battle-8804?page=1; and T.X. Hammes, "Sorry, AirSea Battle Is No Strategy," *National Interest*, August 7, 2013, http://nationalinterest.org/commentary/sorry- airsea-battle-no-strategy-8846.

tion of Chinese airspace and strikes on Chinese land territory, despite the fact that China has vast strategic depth and both a nuclear arsenal and a sufficient conventional arsenal to attack its neighbors. ASB also requires huge investments in high-end defense capabilities in an era of austerity. Ironically, ASB might lead to a reduction in U.S. defense commitments and credibility in Asia, if the United States fails to afford it.

T.X. Hammes denies that ASB is a sensible strategy to defeat A2/AD threats and instead proposes "offshore control," or a blockade against China beyond the range of its A2/AD capabilities, to bring economic pressure to Beijing.[27] Offshore control aims to deter Chinese aggression by showing offshore control capabilities in peacetime, and, if deterrence fails, it creates time for diplomats to negotiate for peace. Offshore control does not include attacks on Chinese land territory, in order to avoid potential nuclear escalation, but instead wages submarine and aerial warfare to deny the PLAN access to its own offshore waters and skies. Offshore control is also cost-effective, as it does not require high-end military platforms.

Offshore control has its own critics, too. For instance, Elbridge Colby wonders whether a distant blockade against China is feasible, as China is an indispensable economic market for many countries.[28] If the United States gives up any option to strike the Chinese mainland, China could invest more into blue water capabilities for sea-lane protection. In addition, China could strike its neighboring countries if they cooperate in an offshore blockade. Without U.S. willingness to destroy the sources of attack on Chinese territory, allies and partners may choose to bandwagon or to acquire an independent nuclear option.

---

27. T.X. Hammes, "Offshore Control: A Proposed Strategy for an Unlikely Conflict," *Strategic Forum*, no. 278 (June 2012); and T.X. Hammes, "Offshore Control Is the Answer," *Proceedings Magazine* 138/12/1, 318 (December 2012).
28. Colby, "Don't Sweat AirSea Battle."

There is a need to fill the gap between ASB and Offshore Control. Jeffrey Kline and Wayne Hughes offer such a solution.[29] Kline and Hughes support ASB as appropriate in a high-end conventional war but propose a war-at-sea strategy to reduce ASB's escalatory nature. The war-at-sea strategy envisions limited naval warfare without striking on land. Like offshore control, the war-at-sea strategy aims to deter Chinese aggression. If deterrence fails, the war-at-sea strategy denies Chinese use of the waters inside the first island chain by using submarines, small guided-missile combat ships, and interdiction along the first island chain. If China strikes U.S. allies and partners, the U.S. military would retaliate with ASB.

The 2014 QDR, which implicitly endorses the war-at-sea strategy, calls for high-end military superiority in the western Pacific. The United States will shrink the existing littoral combat ship (LCS) program and launch a new high-end ship program since the LCSs cannot provide sufficient combat power in Asian waters. The primary challenge for the war-at-sea strategy is how to deter low-intensity conflicts, as China's coercion with paramilitary forces escalates. ASB might deter high-end conflicts while maintaining escalation dominance. But the 2014 QDR fails to provide a sufficient prescription for a counter-coercion strategy.

JAPAN'S NATIONAL SECURITY STRATEGY AND DYNAMIC JOINT DEFENSE FORCE

One of the outcomes from the interaction between China's naval buildup and the U.S. rebalance is the realization that Japan needs to take greater security responsibility in Northeast Asia. Prime Minister Abe has made clear his intention to bolster

---

29. Jeffrey E. Kline and Wayne P. Hughes Jr. , "Between Peace and the Air-Sea Battle: A War at Sea Strategy," *Naval War College Review* 65, no. 4 (Autumn 2012), http://www.usnwc.edu/getattachment/e3120d0c-8c62-4ab7-9342-80597 1ed84f4/Between-Peace-and-the-Air-Sea-Battle--A-War-at-Sea.

security policy with the establishment of the NSS and the NSC and the revision of the NDPG. Abe is determined to protect national territory by investing in the Coast Guard, increasing the defense budget, exercising collective self-defense, and revising the constitution in order to establish a robust national defense force. At the same time, Abe envisions strategic diplomacy and strengthened partnerships with the United States, India, Australia, and other like-minded nations that share universal values in order to recover Japan's economic power and to shape China's behavior in the international arena.

Japan's Strategic Vision
The essence of Abe's strategic vision is the combination of internal balancing (restoring national power to balance the rise of China) and external balancing (allying with like-minded maritime nations to address China's excessive maritime claims).[30] Abe understands the best source of national power is the economy. Abenomics' three arrows address monetary easing, stimulus spending, and growth strategy with structural reforms. Abe is also determined to reform Japan's national security by reversing the decline in defense spending, introducing effective decisionmaking, and relaxing self-imposed restrictions on defense policy.

Abe and his followers envision a coalition among Japan, the United States, India, and Australia—establishing a "democratic security diamond"—as a key enabler for strategic diplomacy.[31] In addition, Abe aims to strengthen ties with the Association of Southeast Asian Nations (ASEAN), visiting all 10 member countries last year and hosting a special Japan-ASEAN summit

30. Michael J. Green, "Japan Is Back: Unbundling Abe's Grand Strategy," Lowy Institute Analysis, December 17, 2013, http://www.lowyinstitute.org/publications/japan-back-unbundling-abes-grand-strategy.
31. Shinzo Abe, "Asia's Democratic Security Diamond," Project Syndicate, December 27, 2002, http://www.project-syndicate.org/commentary/a-strategic-alliance-for-japan-and-india-by-shinzo-abe.

meeting in December 2013. He also visited countries in Europe, the Middle East, and Africa and plans to visit Pacific island nations and Latin America. Abe's strategic diplomacy has two objectives. One is to seek the recovery of Japan's economy by securing energy supplies and opening new markets. Another is to seek understanding for Japanese efforts to address China's attempts to challenge the liberal rule-based order.

Japan's NSS reflects this strategic vision. It recognizes the ongoing power shift between the United States and other emerging powers such as China and India, and calls for a proactive Japanese contribution to peace to maintain the liberal international order. Proactive contribution to peace is antithetical to passive one-nation pacifism. Japan will proactively contribute to the improvement of the regional and global security environment. The NSS puts particular emphasis on the importance of securing the "open and stable ocean."

Good order at sea requires a liberal approach to the international law of the sea, as reflected in the UN Convention on the Law of the Sea (UNCLOS). Such an approach assumes freedom of navigation in maritime commons as a community right, protects sovereign rights of littoral states over maritime resources, and promotes peaceful solutions to maritime disputes. This is the essence of the NSS as a maritime strategy.

Japan is neither going to contain China nor appease Beijing under Chinese military pressure. The rise of China provides both challenges and opportunities to Japan. On one hand, Japan is going to build sufficient defense capabilities and partnerships to discourage Chinese assertiveness, while encouraging Beijing to play more responsible and constructive roles. To that end, Japan needs to establish a robust defensive wall to secure southwestern Japan, while building the capacity of likeminded partners to promote freedom of the seas.

On the other hand, Japan should develop a robust engagement strategy for China. Tokyo should make every effort to communicate and build confidence and trust with Beijing to reduce tension and the risk of clashes and escalation. It is important to work with regional partners because they are concerned about the high tensions between Japan and China and are reluctant to take sides. Japan and China agreed on maritime consultation and crisis communication, and the implementation of those mechanisms is a priority despite China's reluctance. Japan should engage in confidence building with China through multilateral exercises, counterpiracy operations, and humanitarian assistance/disaster response (HA/DR).

Nevertheless, confidence building and crisis management with China are not easy. The problem is not the lack of a mechanism but the lack of a spirit of confidence building and crisis management. The Chinese say trust needs to come before confidence and demands compromise first. Plus, China does not pick up the phone during crises. For instance, the U.S.-China Military Maritime Consultative Agreement (MMCA) has failed to prevent crises such as the recent USS *Cowpens* incident. China does not preserve the spirit of the 1972 U.S.-USSR Incidents at Sea (INCSEA) Agreement and monopolizes the consultations to achieve its political objectives to deny U.S. surveillance in China's claimed EEZs and stop U.S. arms sales to Taiwan.[32] This is why deterrence and hedging still matter.

Japan's Dynamic Joint Defense Force
The concept of a dynamic joint defense force is not new. The December 2010 NDPG emphasized the defense of the Nansei (Southwestern) Islands to meet challenges from China's growing military power.[33] The document, reflecting the

---

32. Pete Pedrozo, "The U.S.-China Incidents at Sea Agreement: A Recipe for Disaster," *Journal of National Security Law & Policy* 6, issue 1 (January 2012).
33. The English text of the NDPG is available at the Ministry of Defense website, http://www.mod.go.jp/e/d_act/ d_policy/national.html; the NDPG was first written in 1976 and revised in 1995, 2004, 2010, and 2013.

changing regional and global security environment, also abandoned the decade-long "static" defense posture and introduced a new concept of "dynamic defense" that envisioned an increased operational level and tempo of the Japan Self-Defense Forces (JSDF).

The dynamic joint defense force is an updated version of the dynamic defense force that calls for further integration of the JSDF. Through the dynamic joint defense force the JSDF will be strengthened in both quantity and quality. Since the defense of the Nansei Islands requires air and maritime superiority, the dynamic joint defense force envisions active and regular surveillance for seamless response to "gray zone scenarios" between peacetime and wartime. Japan plans to introduce the next-generation P-1 patrol aircraft, additional 19,500-ton helicopter-equipped destroyers (DDHs), and unmanned aircraft to enhance surveillance capabilities. Ground-based radar systems in the Nansei Islands will also be enhanced, while early-warning and fighter aircraft based at Naha Air Base will be reinforced.

The Japan Maritime Self-Defense Force (JMSDF) is also protecting against small-scale invasions by strengthening intelligence, surveillance, and reconnaissance (ISR) and antisubmarine warfare (ASW) to defend Japan's surrounding waters. The major area of responsibility for the JMSDF is the East China Sea and the Philippine Sea, or what Japanese naval strategists call the Tokyo-Guam-Taiwan (TGT) Triangle.[34] The new DDH is a primary platform for ASW and it can support amphibious operations. It could be a platform for vertical takeoff and landing (VTOL) aircraft in the future, too. The JMSDF also plans to introduce a new type of smaller, faster, multirole combat ship to be operated in the A2/AD threat environment.

---

34. Tomohisa Takei, "Kaiyoshinjidaini Okeru Kaijojieitai" [Japan Maritime Self-Defense Force in the New Maritime Era], *Hatou*, no. 199 (November 2008).

In addition, the submarine fleet will be increased from 16 to 22. Due to the lack of Chinese ASW capabilities, the expansion of the submarine fleet enhances sea-denial capability vis-à-vis the PLAN. To patrol the waters along southwestern Japan, it is estimated that at least eight submarines are necessary (six for the Okinawa island chain and two for the Bashi Channel). Typically, a boat requires two backups for training and maintenance. Thus a submarine fleet of 24 is ideal, but a fleet of 22 provides more operational flexibility than the current fleet of 16.[35] On the other hand, for the effective use of the reinforced submarine fleet, the JMSDF needs to recruit and train more submariners.

One of the primary objectives of the defense of the Nansei Islands is to prevent China from obtaining air supremacy along the island chain. Seventeen islands in the island chain have civilian airfields, and the Naha, Shimojishima, and Ishigaki airports can operate fighters and large transport aircraft. Those islands need to be protected against Chinese amphibious and airborne invasions so that they can remain open for use by Japanese and American forces. Existing military airport facilities are vulnerable to Chinese ballistic missile attack. Therefore the utilization of commercial facilities on the Southwestern islands is important in terms of dispersion of vulnerability as well.

Ground troops are still indispensable for the defense of the Nansei Islands. The Japan Ground Self-Defense Force (JGSDF) will become lighter and more mobile with Ospreys and light armored vehicles that can be transported by air. The JGSDF will also have an amphibious unit with amphibious assault vehicles; however, the JGSDF plans to purchase the old-generation AAV7 amphibious assault vehicles, which are not suitable for operations in coral reefs, when 85 percent of the Southwestern

35. Masao Kobayashi, "Sensuikan 22 sekitaiseino Kaijoboei" [Maritime Defense under a 22-Submarine Force], *Gunji Kenkyu* [Japan Military Review], December 2011.

Islands are covered by coral reefs. The defense of the Southwestern Island chain requires a new type of amphibious assault vehicle.

Rapid deployment of combat troops, armored vehicles, air-defense units, and ground-to-ship missile launchers is a key enabler of the defense of the Nansei Islands. The introduction of the C-2 next-generation transport aircraft is crucial. Since the Nansei Islands stretch for a thousand miles with limited access facilities, the use of existing commercial air and port facilities is indispensable. The joint use of existing U.S. facilities, the selection of joint supply base sites, and the utilization of civil transportation companies are also urgent. Prepositioning near the Southwestern Islands is another option to consider.

The introduction of amphibious capabilities is expected to be a first step toward a robust joint force. There are two options. One is to establish a permanent joint command with a permanent joint task force.[36] The other is to establish a permanent joint command without a task force.[37] A permanent task force is not a priority. It would be desirable to launch a joint command first and exercise amphibious operations, combining various air-sea-land units as an ad hoc task force. A permanent task force can be organized later, if it is found to be appropriate.

The concept of a dynamic joint defense force makes strategic sense. In essence, it is a Japanese version of an A2/AD strategy along the Nansei Islands. The demonstration of an enhanced defense posture would send a deterrent message to Beijing. It also fits into the war-at-sea strategy to deter Chinese aggression. However, discouraging China's low-intensity aggression in gray zones remains a challenge. The Japanese Coast Guard (JCG), which will be reinforced by 2017, is the first responder

---

36. VAdm. (ret.) Hideaki Kaneda, former commanding officer, Escort Fleet, advocates this option.
37. Lt. Gen. (ret.) Kazuhito Mochida, former commanding general, Western Army, advocates this option.

to such gray zone challenges. Nevertheless, it will continue to be difficult to manage the situation in the East China Sea given China's robust paramilitary ship building program. Moreover, China's increased air operations in the vicinity of Japanese airspace poses an even tougher challenge.

CONCLUSION AND RECOMMENDATIONS

The rise of maritime China has brought about changes to the seas in Asia. Analysis of China's A2/AD strategy through the concepts of fortress fleet and fleet-in-being leads to the conclusion that advances in precision weapons allow the PLAN to assertively expand its operational areas in the Asian littoral. More importantly, the analysis indicates that China could seek strategic stability with the United States, raising the problem of the stability-instability paradox. For Japan and the Unites States, the fundamental challenge is to discourage China's low-intensity assertiveness under the gray zone environment, while maintaining high-end deterrence.

The U.S. rebalance is a geostrategic requirement. The U.S. sea-control fleet and marines-in-dispersion support it. But due to fiscal constraints, its credibility and sustainability are challenged. In order to deter Chinese aggression and reassure allies and partners, the United States needs to implement the rebalance with a robust counter-A2/AD strategy. It is desirable for the United States to maintain flexible deterrence options with ASB; by adopting the war-at-sea strategy, the United States can maintain its influence in the Asia-Pacific.

China's assertiveness in Japan's southwestern front and the U.S. rebalance to Asia require Japan to take a proactive security role. Abe's strategic diplomacy and the introduction of a dynamic joint defense force make strategic sense. Japan is pursuing internal balancing and external balancing at the same time to meet the challenge of rising Chinese power. Economic recovery is the key to internal balancing, while the engagement strategy with China must accompany external balancing. The new defense concept is a war-at-sea strategy with A2/AD capabilities.

The defense of the territorial status quo of the Senkaku Islands and the Nansei Islands in general is the test of the U.S.-Japan alliance. To dissuade China's assertiveness, the two allies need to provide sufficient deterrence and seamlessly respond to gray zone challenges, while assuring regional partners. The revision of the U.S.-Japan Defense Guidelines provides the best opportunity to show the determination of the two allies. Here are some recommendations for the revision:

1. *Adopt a war-at-sea strategy.* To deter Chinese aggression, Japan and the United States should maintain sea-denial capabilities inside the first island chain and sea control beyond the first island chain. ASB provides a wide range of striking options for the war-at-sea strategy, from attack-in-depth to interdiction along the first island chain, all in a high-end A2/AD environment. Denying China's use of the Near Seas and the straits along the first island chain requires cooperation from Australia, India, and ASEAN.

2. *Review the division of labor.* Today's allied division of labor, described as "spear and shield" (Japan provides defensive capabilities and the United States provides offensive capabilities), is obsolete. Japan should take a proactive role in defending its territory with both a short spear and a big shield, while the United States provides a supporting role with a long spear and big eyes to deter escalation. In addition to seamless and constant ISR, primary roles for Japan are tactical air combat, underwater capabilities, ASW, mine/countermine, and air defense operations. Japan's ground-to-ship missile system contributes to

sea denial but the system needs to be upgraded, given the improvements in China's air defense. U.S. primary responsibilities include attack-in-depth by bombers, carrier air wings, and submarines, and unmanned and space-based surveillance. The development of joint and combined ASB operations under the new division of labor makes sense for the efficient use of respective defense capabilities in a period of austerity.[38]

3. *Enhance strategic mobility.* Since the lack of transport capabilities is a common challenge for Japan and the United States, cross-service allied operations—for example, U.S. aircraft transporting Japanese ground troops, or Japanese naval ships transporting U.S. Marines—should be promoted. Utilization of Australian and South Korean platforms is also desirable.

4. *Launch a joint freedom of navigation program.* China's excessive claims in the western Pacific need to be addressed in order for the allies to continue maritime and air surveillance in China's Near Sea. The United States is the only nation that has a freedom of navigation program to challenge littoral countries' excessive maritime claims, but its operational tempo is decreasing. To counter China's legal warfare, Japan and the United States should develop a joint freedom of navigation program. The two militaries should conduct proactive operations to physically challenge China's excessive claims and patrol the East and South China Seas.

5. *Jointly develop new capabilities.* Japan and the United States should jointly develop capabilities such as a new type of amphibious assault vehicle to be operated in

---

38. See Sugio Takahashi, "Counter A2/AD in Japan-US Defense Cooperation: Toward 'Allied Air-Sea Battle,'" Project 2049 Institute Futuregram 12-03, March 2012, http://project2049.net/documents/ counter_a2ad_defense_ cooperation_takahashi.pdf.

coral reefs and a new littoral combat ship, especially for mine warfare operations in high-intensity threat environments. Joint study of antiship ballistic missile defense should also be considered.

6. *Develop a counter-coercion strategy.* Japan and the United States need to work on confidence building and crisis management with China. Nevertheless, to discourage China's low-intensity coercion, Japan and the United States need to develop an asymmetric strategy to shape China's external behavior, while responding to China's gray zone challenges. As long as China continues aggressive actions in the East China Sea, Japan and the United States should deepen their cooperation with Taiwan, given that China claims the Senkaku Islands as part of Taiwan. The Japan-Taiwan fishery agreement of 2013 provided a good example. The allies can also encourage Taiwan to join the Trans-Pacific Partnership (TPP) or facilitate security cooperation, for instance, on cyber defense. Plus, the allies can demonstrate interdiction capabilities vis-à-vis China along the first island chain, as economic growth is a primary source of legitimacy for the Communist Party. ▪

4. JAPAN'S NORTH KOREA STRATEGY: DEALING WITH NEW CHALLENGES

Hiroyasu Akutsu[1]

INTRODUCTION

In December 2013, while North Korea's Kim Jong Un regime was purging Jang Song Thaek, Japan's Shinzo Abe administration established a National Security Council (NSC) and released Japan's first-ever National Security Strategy (NSS) as well as the administration's National Defense Program Guidelines (NDPG). In the two years since the start of the Kim Jong Un regime, North Korea has strengthened its missile and nuclear capabilities, institutionalized its status as a nuclear weapons state, and maintained a belligerent military posture toward the United States, South Korea, and Japan. Despite the regime's occasional signals of openness to dialogue, these events and the purge of Jang reaffirm that the new regime in Pyongyang is another extension of its two predecessors.

Meanwhile in Northeast Asia, China's economic, political, and military rise has been affecting the balance of influence on the Korean peninsula, requiring Japan to review its strategy for North Korea. While China has begun to mitigate the possibility of instability in North Korea by toughening its stance

---

1. The views expressed in this chapter are solely the author's and do not necessarily reflect those of the National Institute for Defense Studies (NIDS).

on the latter's missile program and nuclear adventurism, it has also intensified its "charm offensive" toward South Korea. The so-called South Korea–China "honeymoon," although limited, and the ongoing deterioration of the political and diplomatic atmosphere between Japan and South Korea due to history issues, add other challenges to Japan's strategy for North Korea.

With those challenges in mind, this paper aims to recalibrate Japan's existing policy toward North Korea in light of Japan's new national security strategy. The paper suggests several policies that could contribute to strengthening the Japan-U.S. alliance and Japan-U.S.–South Korea trilateral security cooperation in the future.

JAPAN'S SECURITY POLICY FOR NORTH KOREA AND EMERGING CHALLENGES

The issues concerning North Korea have continued to be a challenge for Japan's current policy and future strategy toward Pyongyang, particularly due to the new regime's belligerent behavior.

New Developments in North Korea

Nearly two years have passed since Kim Jong Un succeeded his father and developments thus far indicate that the nature of the regime and of the tenuous security situation on the Korean peninsula will remain the same. First, after the launch of the advanced *Taepodong II* in December 2012 and the third nuclear test in February 2013, North Korea has articulated "a new strategic line on carrying out economic construction and building nuclear armed forces simultaneously."[2] North Korea says this new strategic line is consistent with Kim Il Sung's strategic line on achieving economic development and national defense si-

---

2. "Report on Plenary Meeting of WPK Central Committee," Korea News Service, March 31, 2013, http://www.kcna.co.jp/item/2013/201303/news31/20130331-24ee.html.

multaneously. In short, Kim Jong Un reiterated that his regime would continue to seek both nuclear weapons and economic prosperity.

Second, North Korea appears to have formulated its first-ever nuclear doctrine. The Supreme People's Assembly passed a law that consolidates North Korea's position as a nuclear weapons state for self-defense. While the law reiterates several of North Korea's previous positions—that the country's nuclear weapons are "not negotiable with the U.S." and serve as a deterrent against the United States—the law also involves several items regarding the Supreme Commander's decision to use nuclear weapons, no first use, management of nuclear material safety, management of nuclear weapons safety, disarmament, and so on. The law may only be an initial preparation for putting forward a more advanced nuclear doctrine in the future. North Korea already stated its status as a nuclear weapons state in the country's revised constitution in April 2012, and the new law can be seen as part of North Korea's institutionalization of that status.

Third, in addition to this declaratory policy, North Korea's move toward the resumption of activities at the nuclear facility in Yongbyon indicates that Pyongyang's determination to maintain its nuclear program is irreversible.

Fourth, regarding North Korea's missile development and activities, Japan and other nations have several concerns. The first is North Korea's development of mid-range *Rodong* missiles that could reach Japan. In addition, North Korea's untested *Musudan* missiles are a growing source of worry among Japan, South Korea, and the United States, not only because the missile's range could allow it to target South Korea, Japan, and Guam but also because it can be launched from mobile launchers and is difficult to detect. Thus, Japan, the United States, and South Korea now have another security concern that Pyongyang can take advantage of in dealing with its three adversaries.

Fifth, North Korea's consolidation of its position as a nuclear weapons state and its provocative and hostile behavior have prompted China to increase its pressure on North Korea, though in a restrained way. The pressure seems to have pushed North Korea to seek dialogue with South Korea, the United States, and Japan. However, as usual, China's limited use of its leverage has not yet made North Korea fully forthcoming.

As for North Korea–China relations, North Korea has long depended on China for economic assistance, and its trade dependence has been increasing continuously. While China is unlikely to pressure North Korea to the extent of destabilizing the Kim regime, China has recently been tougher on North Korea and has used both political and economic/financial levers in the wake of the regime's nuclear test and missile launches. Regarding the purge of Jang Song Thaek, China has officially maintained the principle of noninterference in North Korea's domestic affairs. Even so, China has expressed more explicit concern about North Korea's provocations.

These developments indicate that the Six-Party Talks have become even less effective, and that the prospect for any substantial international dialogue with North Korea on denuclearizing is still dim. Any word or deed that makes North Korea believe that its status as a *de facto* nuclear weapons state is acknowledged would further embolden North Korea.

Japan's Security Policy for North Korea
In Northeast Asia, the Korean peninsula and the Taiwan Strait have long been Japan's two most important geostrategic locations, with the stability of each having direct ramifications for Japan's security. These two locations have likewise been recognized as vital to Japan in the Japan-U.S. Security Treaty. Given

this, maintaining and advancing peace and security in those two areas and beyond in Northeast Asia remains an essential part of Japan's core security interests.

Japan has based its North Korea policy mainly on the 2002 Pyongyang Declaration, which utilizes "pressure (or deterrence) and dialogue" to address the highly prioritized abduction issue along with missile and nuclear concerns (see Table 1). Japan has expressed its determination to bring those issues to a complete resolution. To do so, the Abe administration has been trying to enhance strategic communications with North Korea while retaining a solid deterrence posture against its military provocations.

Table 1: Framework of Japan's Existing Policy Response to North Korea's Belligerence

Pressure/Deterrence	Dialogue
• Japan's own response and denial capabilities	• Bilateral: Japan–North Korea direct talks
• Japan-U.S. alliance-based cooperation, including Ballistic Missile Defense (BMD)	• Multilateral: Six-Party Talks
• Japan-U.S.–South Korea Trilateral Security Cooperation	
• Proliferation Security Initiative (PSI)	
• Economic/Financial Sanctions (UN/Individual)	

Japan's "pressure" on North Korea has been focused on deterrence by denial, which involves ballistic missile defense (BMD), maritime security, and full cooperation with the United States. The pressure approach also includes deterrence by punishment in the form of restrictions on nonmilitary trade and financial sanctions. North Korea's launch of long-range missiles in 2009 led the prime minister's security advisory group and Japanese policymakers in the major political parties to forge a consensus in favor of punitive measures including striking the adversary's bases. Japan aims to develop its own capability to deal with North Korea's missile threats, a point that will be discussed in great detail later.

Japan's threat perception of, and policy direction toward, North Korea are basically consistent. In fact, regarding North Korea's ballistic missiles, the NSS states:

> North Korea's ballistic missiles development, including those with ranges covering the mainland of the US, along with its continued attempts to miniaturize nuclear weapons for warheads and equipping them to ballistic missiles, substantially aggravate the threat to the security of the region, including Japan. These concerns pose a serious challenge to the entire international community from the viewpoint of the non-proliferation of WMD and related materials.[3]

The NSS also articulates Japan's North Korea strategy as follows:

> With regard to the issues of North Korea, Japan will cooperate closely with relevant countries to urge North Korea to take concrete actions towards its denuclearization and other goals, based on the Joint Statement of the Six-Party Talks and rel-

3. Japan's National Security Strategy, 2013, 25, http://www.cas.go.jp/jp/siryou/131217anzenhoshou/nss-e.pdf.

evant UN Security Council (UNSC) Resolutions.
Concerning Japan-North Korea relations, Japan
will endeavor to achieve a comprehensive resolution of outstanding issues of concern, such as
the abduction, nuclear and missile issues, in accordance with the Japan-North Korea Pyongyang
Declaration. In particular, it is the basic recognition of Japan that normalization of relations with
North Korea will not be possible without resolving
the abduction issue. Japan will make every effort
to realize the safety and prompt return of all ab-
ductees at the earliest possible date, investigate
the truth regarding the abductions, and transfer
those who executed the abductions.[4]

Thus, Japan's basic policy direction and framework for North
Korea have persisted for the past 12 years, and in the meantime,
North Korea's missile and nuclear capabilities have only progressed. At the same time, China's economic and military rise
has affected the balance of influence on the Korean peninsula.

The Emerging Challenges
The new developments within the North Korean regime and
China's tactical adjustments regarding its policies toward both
North and South Korea have produced more challenges than
opportunities for Japan's existing North Korea policy.

First, North Korea's nuclear and missile capabilities have
progressed and tools for provocations have increased, including assets for conducting cyberattacks. The Japan-U.S.
alliance's main focus has been North Korea's ballistic missile
threat. The alliance's BMD program has been updated accordingly to respond to North Korea's heightened capability and
technological progression. Japan has always been under the

---

4. Ibid., 12.

threat of North Korea's *Rodong* mid-range ballistic missile. With the rapid progress of North Korea's missile capability, the United States and Japan are forced to accelerate their co-operation to advance the quality of their BMD systems. In the wake of North Korea's third nuclear test in February 2013, the United States decided to deploy a second TPY-2 radar to Japan. Both Japan and the United States agreed to promote this plan. Japan and the United States also already agreed to upgrade the Guidelines for Defense Cooperation to include space and cyberspace security by the end of 2014. These are encouraging developments in the context of the Japan-U.S. alliance, but Japan needs to move even faster to improve its own defense capabilities.

Second, with China rising in both economic and military dimensions, North Korea's material dependence on China is increasing rapidly. By now, it is clear that China puts pressure on North Korea when it thinks it needs to, but China will not destabilize the North Korean regime. Also, despite South Korea's opposition to China's sudden and unilateral announcement of an East China Sea air defense identification zone (ADIZ) in November and the Japan-ROK naval exercise in December 2013, history issues between Japan and South Korea have led to a closer relationship between China and South Korea. These developments demonstrate that Japan has to reevaluate the best means to improve security cooperation with South Korea.

Third, a related challenge is the political limitations on Japan–South Korea security cooperation that have affected Japan-U.S.–South Korea trilateral security cooperation. Given North Korea's continued military development, especially in advanced missile capabilities, the need is increasing to deepen the linkage between the Japan-U.S. alliance and the U.S.–South Korea alliance, especially in the area of BMD.

ADDITIONAL POLICY PROPOSALS FOR JAPAN

Thus, Japan's North Korea strategy has been consistent and stable for the past 12 years, but because of the growth of North Korea's military capabilities as well as China's rise and its influence on the Korean peninsula, Japan has to make necessary tactical adjustments. As mentioned at the outset, Japan has established a National Security Council (NSC) and released a National Security Strategy (NSS) and new National Defense Program Guidelines (NDPG). These moves, including the decision to strengthen the Japan Maritime Self-Defense Force's *Aegis* system, indicate Japan's will to continue its own security efforts. However, there are several other issues Japan should address swiftly.

Enhance Deterrence / Extended Deterrence

I. *Solve the issue of Japan's collective self-defense right.* First, Japan should solve the long-overdue issue of the collective self-defense right in which Japan has maintained that the nation has that right but cannot exercise it because of constitutional constraints. This issue can be solved either by changing the Liberal Democratic Party's existing interpretation of the right or through constitutional revisions. The latter will be time-consuming. From the viewpoint of strategic efficiency, an interpretational change is more desirable. The United States, Japan's most important and only formal ally, has been kept waiting for a long time, so the sooner the better.

Japan's resolution of this issue should be welcomed by South Korea as well. Since the mid-1990s, Track 2 security experts in Japan and South Korea have discussed the issue intensively and have even conducted simulations in the wake of North Korea's conventional and nuclear threats. These discussions and exercises have helped leading South

Korean security intellectuals to understand the importance of Japan having this right. There is no reason that new generations of South Korean intellectuals should be unable to understand how helpful Japan could be to supporting the U.S.–South Korea alliance, Japan-U.S.–South Korea trilateral security cooperation, and Japan–South Korea bilateral security cooperation.

2. *Enhance Japan's own response and deterrence capabilities.* Second, as briefly suggested above, Japan is trying to enhance its own capability to respond to North Korea's missile threat more effectively. The new NDPG states the following:

> Based on appropriate role and mission sharing between Japan and the U.S., in order to strengthen the deterrent of the Japan-U.S. Alliance as a whole through enhancement of Japan's own deterrent and response capability, Japan will study a potential form of response capability to address the means of ballistic missile launches and related facilities, and take means as necessary.[5]

Japan is still studying such a capability, but Japan should more swiftly move to develop the capability as North Korea develops its missile capabilities rapidly. This would help further strengthen U.S. extended deterrence, including the U.S nuclear umbrella, provided to Japan.

3. *Enhance ballistic missile defense (BMD).* Third, the further enhancement of Japan's role in the U.S.-led BMD initiative will strengthen both Japan's overall defense capability and the U.S. extended deterrence, including the U.S. nuclear umbrella in Northeast Asia. In recent years, Japan has made progress

---

5. Japan's National Defense Program Guidelines for FY 2014 and Beyond, 2013, 20, http://www.mod.go.jp/j/approach/agenda/guideline/2014/pdf/20131217_e2.pdf.

in developing its capabilities to play an appropriate role in the initiative. As mentioned above, the new NDPG states that Japan will increase the current number of *Aegis* ships from six to seven and introduce PAC-3 MSE. Japan should continue these efforts to keep up with North Korean missile development.

"Dialogue" on Abduction

The Abe administration has been searching for an opportunity to reach out to North Korea regarding the abduction issue. The NSS articulates the administration's strong determination to the resolve this issue:

> North Korea's abduction is a grave issue affecting Japan's sovereignty as well as the lives and safety of Japanese nationals. It is an urgent issue for the Government of Japan to resolve under its responsibility and a universal issue for the international community to address as a violation of fundamental human rights.[6]

The administration seems to have started some sort of strategic communications with North Korea in 2013. Even as North Korea sends positive signals to Japan on talking about this issue, its basic stance toward Japan is still very hostile. Japan needs to continue patient testing of North Korea's willingness for serious discussions. In so doing, however, Japan needs to coordinate with the U.S. and South Korea to better gather useful information inside North Korea and to prepare for more effective engagement with North Korea in the future.

Japan–South Korea Security Cooperation

Stronger Japan–South Korea security ties are essential to Japan's North Korea strategy. Japan should pursue the following to enhance its cooperation with South Korea.

---

6. Japan's National Security Strategy, 2013, 12.

   1. *Maintain minimum security cooperation with South Korea.*
       Japan should encourage South Korea to focus on
       pragmatic bilateral security cooperation. Japan-
       South Korea political and diplomatic relations
       have been deteriorating, and the politicization and
       institutionalization of the history issue has made
       cooperation between the two democracies more difficult.

   One positive sign is that pragmatic security cooperation
   between the two countries is still alive. As demonstrated
   in the Tables 2 and 3, Japan-U.S.–South Korea and Japan–
   South Korea joint naval exercises have been conducted
   even after the cancellation of the signing of the Japan–
   South Korea General Security of Military Information
   Agreement (GSOMIA) in 2012.

   In particular, the Japan-ROK joint naval exercise in
   December 2013 is notable symbolically given that it was
   conducted after China's sudden and unilateral announcement of an ADIZ in the East China Sea.

   It is also clear that while Japan–South Korea joint exercises might have been restrained or conducted in a
   low-key way, Japan-U.S.–South Korea joint exercises appear orchestrated to fill gaps in Japan–South Korea joint
   exercises. This indicates that the U.S. role is important
   in bringing Japan and South Korea together when the
   political atmosphere between them is not ideal. It also
   demonstrates that the Japan-U.S.–South Korea trilateral
   is indispensable. Japan should continue to seek U.S. cooperation in this area.

Table 2: Japan-ROK-U.S. Joint Naval Exercises (Disclosed Exercises)

Date	Exercise Activities	Location
August 6, 2009	Search and Rescue (SAREX)	Hawaii
June 21–22, 2012	SAREX, inspection, etc.	South of Korean peninsula
August 8–9, 2012	SAREX, inspection, communications, etc.	Hawaii
May 15, 2013	SAREX, inspection, etc.	West of Kyushu
October 10–11, 2013	SAREX, supply, etc.	West of Kyushu
December 11–13, 2013	Shooting, inspection	Gulf of Aden

Sources: *Defense of Japan* (2005–13), Japanese newspapers, etc.

Table 3: Japan-ROK Joint Naval SAREX (Disclosed Exercises)

Date	Location
August 5, 1999	Between Sasebo and Cheju
September 12, 2002	Southwest of Tsushima
August 6, 2003	West of Tsushima
August 26, 2005	Southwest of Tsushima
June 20, 2007	East of Cheju
July 7, 2009	North of Oki Islands
November 12–13, 2011	Northeast of Tsushima
December 12, 2013	West of Kyushu

Sources: *Defense of Japan* (2005–13), Japanese newspapers, etc.

2.   *Alleviate South Korea's "G-2 Dilemma."* Japan should help ameliorate South Korea's "G-2 dilemma"—concerns about a U.S.-China accommodation at the expense of U.S. allies and partners in East Asia—especially given the recent discussions of a "new type of major country/great power relationship" between the United States and China. South Korea feels caught between economic dependence on China, on the one hand, and security reliance on the United States, on the other. While the U.S.–South Korea alliance has been strengthened, South Korea is also encouraging China's charm offensive by emphasizing a "South Korea–China honeymoon" to marginalize Japan. Japan should strive to help South Korea get out of the "G2" mindset by closely working with the United States to keep South Korea on the right side of the strategic front. Toward that end, Japan should ask the United States to further articulate what it means by "operationalizing a new model of major power relations" in terms of denuclearizing North Korea. This term seems to have reinforced the G-2 dilemma in South Korea and has also kept many Japanese policy intellectuals guessing about Washington's China policy.

3.   *Sign GSOMIA and revive ACSA discussions.* Related to the previous suggestion, the new NDPG declares that Japan will make an effort to establish a foundation for closer cooperation with South Korea, for example by concluding the General Security of Military Information Agreement as well as an Acquisition and Cross-Servicing Agreement (ACSA). Japan should keep requesting that South Korea accede to these agreements. This has been endorsed by many experts in Japan and the United States, and it cannot be emphasized enough.

4.   *Shift from "common values" to "common strategic vision and objectives."* Japan and South Korea already agreed on

common values in the late 1990s; it is time for both countries to articulate a common strategic vision and common objectives. It is not too early for Japan to start working on that vision and those objectives. These objectives and vision should include the following:

- Japan and South Korea should work jointly to enhance the U.S. extended deterrent to maintain stability on the Korean peninsula and in Northeast Asia;

- Japan and South Korea should cooperate to maintain and strengthen the U.S. presence in Northeast Asia and beyond;

- Japan and South Korea should continue to cooperate to deter North Korea from developing and proliferating weapons of mass destruction (WMD);

- Japan and South Korea should continue to cooperate with other U.S. allies, such as Australia, and like-minded democracies, such as India, to ensure stability in the Indo-Asia-Pacific and beyond; and

- Japan and South Korea should cooperate to promote democracy and market mechanisms on the Korean peninsula and in Northeast Asia.

These are only basic examples that should be further developed in the future. Additionally, it would be even more encouraging if both countries began to discuss a joint security declaration between them modeled on the joint security declarations Japan and South Korea already have with Australia.

5. *Promote pragmatism over emotionalism.* Finally, Japan and South Korea should at least contain the issue of history by agreeing not to politicize the issue in the spirit of sensible pragmatism over emotionalism. There is a precedent

from 2004 in which South Korea and China "contained" the issues of history by agreeing on the so-called five principles to avoid politicization.

In the case of the history between Japan and South Korea, the two countries have conducted joint studies of history from 2002 to 2005 and 2007 to 2010. The Japanese and South Korean historians involved have not made progress, but it seems better that historians and experts argue with one another than to allow political tensions to hinder pragmatic security cooperation between the two countries. From this point of view, another round of joint historical study might be useful in relieving historical emotionalism.

Japan-U.S.–South Korea Trilateral Security Cooperation
New developments in North Korea confirm the continued importance of the deterrent capabilities of the Japan-U.S. alliance and the U.S.–South Korea alliance and of direct security cooperation between Japan and South Korea. While maintaining and strengthening allied vigilance regarding North Korea's nuclear capabilities, the three partners should enhance their intelligence, surveillance, and reconnaissance (ISR) and BMD capabilities and conduct joint training and exercises to deal with North Korea's missile launches and other hostile activities.

One of the most potentially dangerous North Korean capabilities is its untested *Musudan* missile, whose 2,500- to 4,000-km range covers South Korea, Japan, and Guam. Responding to this problem will require closer coordination among the three partners as well as between Japan and South Korea. While U.S. extended deterrence against North Korea remains strong, North Korea's overconfidence in its nuclear deterrence capabilities may trigger the stability-instability paradox. This suggests that in addition to trilateral cooperation, enhancing bilateral Japan-South Korea ties is necessary. In addition to the revival of the GSOMIA process and discussion on ACSA, involving South Korea in the U.S.-led BMD program would be valuable. South Korea wants to develop its own kill chain and BMD systems, but more intensive trilateral discussion on this issue would be helpful.

To date, the United States has been the only bridge connecting the Japan-U.S. and U.S.-ROK alliances. In practice, the connection between these two alliances can be seen in the form of Japan-U.S.-South Korea trilateral security cooperation in dealing with North Korea. Trilateral cooperation among Japan, the United States, and South Korea should follow the examples of the Trilateral Policy Oversight and Coordination Group (TCOG) and the Korean Peninsula Energy Development Organization (KEDO) in the 1990s. Revitalizing the senior-level trilateral policy coordination mechanism would also be useful for synchronizing the three partners' engagement with North Korea. The TCOG was possible because of the so-called Perry Process and a comprehensive review of America's North Korea policy. The United States should keep these examples in mind.

The fact that both bilateral Japan–South Korea and trilateral Japan-U.S.–South Korea military exercises have been conducted and defense exchanges have been maintained despite the worsening of political and diplomatic relations between Japan and South Korea indicates that Japan and South Korea know the detriments of severing security ties between the two "virtual allies," and know that some of the fundamental parameters of defense relations should not be dictated by what is reported in the media.

In addition to sustaining various kinds of financial and economic sanctions on North Korea, the Proliferation Security Initiative (PSI) should also be further utilized to strengthen allied efforts against North Korea's proliferation activities.

Cooperation among Other U.S. Allies

Finally, security cooperation among multiple U.S. allies and like-minded countries in the Asia-Pacific would be useful for deterring North Korea's military provocations. It would also help stabilize the whole region if a contingency occurs because those allies can actually provide operational capabilities to deal with such a crisis.

The most effective form of such cooperation would be among Japan, South Korea, Australia, and the United States. These like-minded democracies are not only U.S. allies but they have bilateral joint security agreements among themselves (except for the Japan–South Korea leg). Military exercises and joint PSI initiatives by the United States and its allies could further develop the habit of cooperation among them and encourage collective balancing in Northeast Asia.

CONCLUSION

Japan's first-ever NSS indicates that there is no significant change in the basic direction of Japan's strategy, but this paper suggests adjusting the strategy by adding proposals for several new policy initiatives. The NSS is designed to determine Japan's strategy for the next decade, but it is supposed to be revised whenever necessary given the uncertain security environment. Japan's strategy should also be reviewed through careful observation of North Korea's behavior and the future security environment surrounding the Korean peninsula.

What is rather certain, however, is that the Japan-U.S. alliance and the Japan-U.S.–South Korea trilateral continue to be the most effective tools for Japan's North Korea strategy. Japan should continue to focus on strengthening its capabilities and roles in its security cooperation with the United States and South Korea, while also striving to enhance its own defense capabilities. ∎

5. ENHANCING ENERGY RESILIENCE: CHALLENGING TASKS FOR JAPAN'S ENERGY POLICY

Yoshikazu Kobayashi[1]

INTRODUCTION

Three years after the 3-11 earthquake in Japan, the cabinet approved the new Basic Energy Plan (BEP) this spring. The new BEP, a product of lengthy and heated discussions among policy planners, academics, and business leaders, calls nuclear energy "an important base-load power supply source" for the future of Japan's energy supply, and provides fundamental policy direction for other energy sources such as coal, oil, natural gas, electricity, and renewable energy. The new BEP will serve as the framework for developing and implementing specific policies for each energy source.

1. The views provided in this paper are solely those of the author and do not represent the views of the author's affiliated institute. In preparing for this research, the author is grateful for the input of Mr. Daisuke Asano, Professor Akira Morita, Mr. Takahisa Hiruma, Professor Masahiro Akiyama, and Gen. Yoshiaki Yano (Ret.) through discussions in the working group established as part of the research project, *Kakkoku no Energy Kankei Kigyou Kikann no Doukou wo Fumaeta Sekiyu Kanrenn Sangyou no Bunseki* [Analysis of Petroleum Industry based on other countries' energy industry and organizations' activities] commissioned by the Ministry of Economy, Trade, and Industry in the fiscal year 2012. The author is solely responsible for all faults, mistakes, and shortcomings that remain in this paper.

In light of these developments, this paper reviews Japan's policy challenges from the viewpoint of enhancing resilience. The main theme is that Japan must enhance its energy supply system's resilience against supply shocks. The use of the term "resilience" has become common since the 3-11 earthquake. However, resilience has been discussed mainly in the context of "hard" disciplines, such as civil engineering and disaster prevention, and less so in the context of securing energy supply systems, other than in just a few studies.[2] Because the risk of supply disruption cannot be reduced to zero, strengthening prompt recovery capabilities should have more significance in Japan's energy policies. The objective of this paper is to apply resilience to energy security policy and to consider future policy directions. Section 1 considers the concept of resilience in the energy supply system. Section 2 discusses why Japan needs to enhance its resilience in its energy supply. Section 3 provides specific policy measures to upgrade impact mitigation and achieve a more resilient energy supply structure. Section 4 identifies potential items of bilateral energy cooperation between Japan and the United States.

RESILIENCE IN ENERGY SUPPLY

Resilience as a term was used originally in mathematics to describe the ability to return to a stable condition. The term then became used to describe the quality of material in the field of civil engineering. Resilience in civil engineering indicates to what extent a certain material can be bent by external physical force, how quickly the material recovers its original condition, and how much force finally breaks the material. These three

---

2. Such exceptions are Council on Competitiveness-Nippon, *Rejiriento Economi no Soushutsu* [Creation of Resilient Economy], March 2013; Ministry of Economy, Trade, and Industry, *Kakkoku no Energy Kankei Kigyou Kikann no Doukou wo Fumaeta Sekiyu Kanrenn Sangyou no Bunseki* [Analysis of Petroleum Industry based on the other countries' energy industry and organizations' activities], March 2013.

properties are respectively referred to as resistance, elasticity, and robustness.[3] Resilience measures the longer-term sustainability of a certain material beyond simple physical robustness.

Resilience is used in psychological studies as well. A resilient person has mental toughness against external pressures as well as a high ability to adapt to hardship, particularly poverty.[4] Resistance against external hardship and the capability to turn given adverse conditions into more positive and acceptable ones are the most important features of resilience in psychological studies. In this sense, psychological resilience focuses more on flexibility than simple toughness in evaluating a person's mental characteristics.

Social sciences, such as economics and management studies, also deal with resilience. In macroeconomics, a country's resilience is defined by its capability to return to an economic growth track after an external (and often unavoidable) shock. Just as in psychology, adaptability to macroeconomic adversity is a key determinant of resilience.[5]

Similarly, a firm with the capacity to adapt to an adverse change in its management environment and to devise and

3. Per Bodin and Bo L. B. Wiman, "Resilience and other stability concepts in ecology," *ESS Bulletin* 2, no. 2 (2004): 33–34; C.S. Holling, "Engineering Resilience versus Ecological Resilience," in *Foundations of Ecological Resilience*, ed. Peter Schulze (Washington, DC: National Academies Press, 1996), 32–33; Patrick Martin-Breen and J. Marty Anderies, "Resilience: A Literature Review," Rockefeller Foundation, September 2011, http://www.rockefellerfoundation.org/media/download/a63827c7-f22d-495c-a2ab-99447a8809ba.
4. Tuppett M. Yates, Byron Egeland, and Alan Sroufe, "Rethinking Resilience: A Developmental Process Perspective," in *Resilience and Vulnerability*, ed. Suniya S. Luthar (Cambridge: Cambridge University Press, 2003), 249–50; Michael Rutter, "Implications of Resilience Concepts for Scientific Understanding," *Annals of New York Academy of Sciences*, 1094 (2006), 1–2.
5. Romain Duval, Jørgen Elmeskov, and Lukas Vogel, "Structural Policies and Economic Resilience to Shocks," Working Paper No. 567, OECD (2007), 2–3.

implement a new business model to overcome this hardship is regarded as a highly resilient firm in the field of management studies.[6] Managerial resilience features not only a simple adaptability but also a capacity to create innovation and turn a crisis into a business opportunity.[7]

Although its definition and implications vary, several characteristics of resiliency are common across disciplines.[8] First, resilience in all the aforementioned disciplines assumes the presence of an adverse external pressure (physical, psychological, economic, or managerial) that is often unexpected and unavoidable but nevertheless must be overcome. Thus, resilience is not a passive concept that addresses only how to avoid risk; it is a proactive concept that also explores how to face risk and how to respond to unavoidable negative events.

Second, and relatedly, resilience focuses on mitigating crisis impacts and adapting to negative events rather than risk mitigation. If an adverse situation can be anticipated, preparing for it and strengthening the ability to manage risks is certainly important. However, because negative shocks often happen unexpectedly, ensuring dynamic flexibility and adaptability is also an essential element of resilience.

Third, the time needed to recover is also critical in measuring resilience. In civil engineering or economics, the time needed to return to an original state determines the quality of

---

6. Gary Hamel and Liisa Valikangas, "The Quest for Resilience," *Harvard Business Review*, September 2003, 3.

7. Ibid.

8. The Rockefeller Foundation summarizes common aspects among usage of the term resilience as follows: "Like all words in circulation for so long, there are variations in its usage. But across the academic disciplines and indeed in common parlance there is a universal meaning of the term that includes the ability to respond to or bounce back from stress and shocks in a healthy and functional way." Rockefeller Foundation, *Embracing Change: Building Social, Economic, and Environmental Resilience* (New York: Rockefeller Foundation, June 2012), 2.

material and the economic competitiveness of a country, respectively.

Thus, assuming that unavoidable negative events will happen, enhancing resistance to external shocks, mitigating impacts caused by such events, and improving the capacity to recover in a prompt manner are the three essential elements of resilience. Figure 1 depicts these aspects conceptually.

Figure 1: Graphical Representation of Resilience

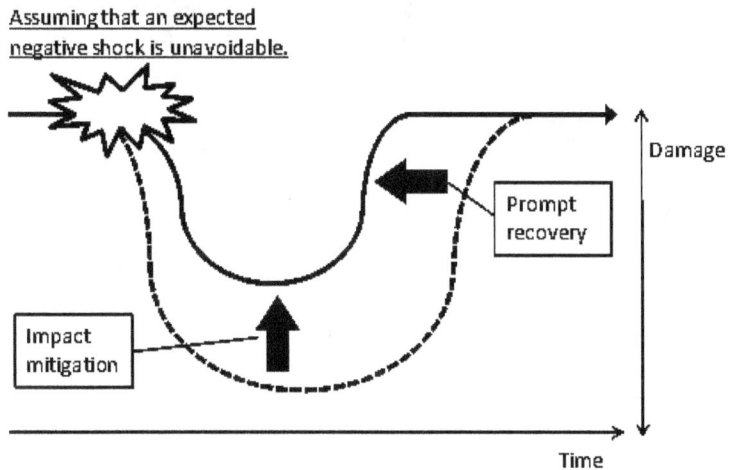

Source: Akira Morita, "*Shimin Shakai no Anzen Hoshou*" [Security of Civil Society], November 2012, http://salix.at.webry.info/201211/article_1. html (modified by author).

Resilience in an energy supply system, hereafter referred to as energy resilience, also employs these three aspects. Adverse events could include unexpected supply disruptions from oil and gas exporting countries, logistical problems in maritime transport of energy resources, severe accidents in the power generation sector, or excessive fluctuation of energy prices. Given these issues, Japan needs to strengthen its ability to mitigate impacts (risk management) and recover promptly (crisis management) to ensure a stable energy supply.

Japan's traditional energy security policy has placed a great emphasis on impact mitigation in addressing energy resilience. The foundation of present Japanese energy security policy was formed in the 1970s, when Japan experienced two oil crises. The largest challenge for energy security policymakers at that time was making Japan more immune to external disruptions to oil supply and accompanying price fluctuations. In order to achieve this goal, Japan worked intensively to reduce its dependence on oil, particularly in the power generation sector. Japan began to pursue nuclear energy, liquefied natural gas (LNG), and coal-fired power plants. As a result of efforts over the last several decades, the share of oil-fired power generation dropped sharply from 73.2 percent in 1973 to just 8.5 percent in 2012.

Japan has also made significant strides in energy conservation. Japan's energy intensity (energy consumption required to generate a unit of economic growth) has improved from 0.165 tons oil equivalent per one thousand dollars GDP in 1973 to 0.096 tons oil equivalent per one thousand dollars GDP in 2012, now among the lowest in the world. Japan has also built significant oil stockpiles retained by both the government and private companies. Total stockpiles exceed a 180-day equivalent of Japan's domestic oil sales. In this sense, Japan's efforts have successfully made the country's defenses against energy supply risk more robust.

These policies, however, are all impact mitigation measures implemented before a certain supply risk event happens. Possible responses once a risk to supply has occurred are less well developed. This lack of emphasis on crisis management has led to the idea that a serious crisis can be avoided as long as sufficient impact mitigation measures are undertaken. This so-called "safety myth" is often cited as one of the root causes of the accident at the Fukushima Daiichi Nuclear Power Plant. This myth arose from various factors, but the imbalance of emphasis on risk prevention versus emergency response is one important factor.[9] Of course, this does not mean impact mitigation measures are not important. As explained in section 3, they continue to be a major part of efforts to enhance energy resilience and need to be reinvigorated. Even so, given the changing environment in international energy markets as well as the experience from the 3-11 earthquake, Japan's energy security policy should focus more on emergency response as a way to enhance reliance.

WHY RESILIENCE IS RELEVANT TO JAPAN'S CURRENT ENERGY SUPPLY

Resilience is increasingly relevant to and significant for today's Japanese energy policy for several reasons. First, there are growing geopolitical uncertainties in the international energy supply. Japan depends on imports for most of its fossil fuel supply. In particular, its sources for oil supply are concentrated in the Middle East.[10] Political turmoil and civil unrest triggered by a series of civil movements beginning in 2011 (the so-called

9. Safety myth issues have been pointed out as one of root causes of the Fukushima Daiichi nuclear power plant accident. See *Investigation Committee on the Accident at the Fukushima Nuclear Power Stations Final Report*, July 2012, 527–28; Rebuild Japan Initiative Forum, *Fukushima Genpatsu Jiko Dokuritsu Kensho Iinkai Chousa Kenshou Houkokusho* [Research Report by Independent Investigation Commission of Fukushima Nuclaer Power Plant Accident] (Discover 21, March 2012), 323–34. Such a myth was also needed to assure local residents near nuclear power plants.

10. Dependence on Middle East crude oil as a percentage of total imports was 85.1 percent in 2011 and 83.2 percent in 2012, according to Keizai Sangyou Shou [Ministry of Economy, Trade, and Industry], *Shigen Enerugi-Tokei* [Resource and Energy Statistics].

Arab Spring) have continued in several countries, such as Syria and Libya. Although there are signs of improvement in the relationship between the P5+1 and Iran since the November 2013 Geneva Agreement, ties are still strained. If no significant progress is made before the expiration of the agreement in July 2014, the United States and European Union might impose additional sanctions and political tensions could deteriorate further. Geopolitical uncertainties surrounding the Middle East continue to mount, so Japan must increasingly guard against an unexpected supply shock originating from the region.

Second, the demand side of the international energy market brings another risk to Japan's external supply. Energy demand growth from emerging countries will continue to heighten the risk of tightening market balances and price hikes. The Institute of Energy Economics, Japan (IEEJ) predicts that Asian energy demand will grow by 1.8 times from 2011 to 2040. The annual average growth rate will be 2.5 percent, far exceeding the world average at 1.6 percent.[11] Another aspect that should not be ignored is Asia's increasing import dependency. IEEJ predicts that by 2040, 80 percent of Asia's oil supply will come from imports. Emerging countries that require more energy imports may become more assertive in their foreign policies. Regardless of the extent to which energy demand from and imports to these countries actually grow, perceived supply insecurity could increase. Needless to say, political tensions in the South China Sea and East China Sea in the last few years are caused in part by regional powers' quest for energy resources and the desire to guarantee stable navigation routes for oil and gas.

Third, the experience of the 3-11 earthquake and the Fukushima Daiichi accident has reinforced the importance for Japan of preparing for an unexpected and even unimaginable event. Due to its geography, Japan is susceptible to various natural disasters such as typhoons, volcanic eruptions, heavy rain or

---

11. Institute of Energy Economics, Japan, *Asia / World Energy Outlook 2013*, October 2013.

snow, tsunamis, and earthquakes. In addition to natural disasters, new risks to energy supply systems, such as cyberattacks and pandemics, are also emerging. This changing environment has increased the vulnerability of Japan's energy supply. Potential supply disruption scenarios have therefore expanded significantly and it is more difficult to predict what scenarios might occur and to prepare for them adequately. This reality calls for Japan to develop more thorough and comprehensive emergency response measures in addition to its efforts to anticipate likely scenarios and to develop ways to mitigate the risks attendant in those scenarios. In other words, the emergency recovery aspect of energy supply resilience needs to be strengthened.

POLICY ITEMS TO ENHANCE ENERGY RESILIENCE

Japan can enhance its energy resilience by upgrading impact mitigation measures as well as strengthening prompt recovery measures. Policy initiatives to achieve these goals are summarized in Table 1.

Table 1: Policy Items to Enhance Energy Resilience

Impact mitigation	Utilizing safe nuclear power plants
	Diversifying supply sources
	Diversifying energy pricing references
	Optimizing thermal power generation sources
	Taking pragmatic action on climate change
Prompt recovery	Guarding free and open energy market transactions
	Guaranteeing free and open international maritime order
	Developing prompt and adaptive government decisionmaking
	Implementing nationwide and interagency exercises
	Mobilizing stockpile

Source: Author.

Utilizing Safe Nuclear Power Plants

One of the primary elements in enhancing Japan's energy resilience is, as discussed above, upgrading impact mitigation measures. The first and most important task in this regard is to verify the operational safety of Japan's nuclear power plants. Although 50 nuclear units currently exist in Japan, as of February 2014 all units are not operational as the Nuclear Regulatory Authority (NRA) conducts its approval process.[12] Due to the loss of nuclear power generation, an additional 3.6 trillion yen was spent to increase purchases of alternative power generation fuels such as LNG and oil. This means, with a Japanese population of approximately 120 million, an average four-person household has to pay an *additional* $1,200 per year for fuel imports. Such a large import consumer burden is certainly damaging Japan's economic viability and worsening its vulnerability to external supply shocks and energy price hikes.

Resuming nuclear power generation is never an easy task. Even though power companies could obtain approval from the NRA for several units to operate, the real hurdle is to obtain public acceptance of and confidence in nuclear safety. Public trust toward safety (*Anshin*, in Japanese) is quite different from objectively and scientifically confirmed safety (*Anzen*, in Japanese).[13] In order to recover the public's trust in nuclear en-

---

12. The Fukushima accident raised severe criticism of the Japanese regulatory framework where essentially the same ministry (Ministry of Economy, Trade, and Industry) oversees safety oversight as well as promotes nuclear energy development. A new independent regulatory body, the Nuclear Regulatory Authority (NRA), was set up in September 2012, and the authority published a new safety standard in July 2013 to reflect the experience of the Fukushima accident. As of February 2014, 16 nuclear units are applying to restart operations, but NRA approval has been delayed.

13. The difference of these two concepts (*Anshin* and *Anzen*) has been a major research topic among the Japanese social psychologists even before the Fukushima accident. See Kazuya Nakayachi, *Anzen, demo Anshin dekinai: Shinrai wo meguru Shinri Gaku* [Being safe, but not being felt safe, psychology of trust], Chikuma Shobo, 2008, 12–15.

ergy, a strong, independent, and capable regulatory authority is necessary. Appropriate regulation and oversight of nuclear power plant operations are needed to show the public that the operations of nuclear power plants are controlled sufficiently. The NRA is expected to become such a reliable institution.

Besides the establishment of a proper regulatory body, changing perceptions of risk control are needed as a soft measure. In the past, the government and power companies have both tried to ensure that no risk of any accident at plants exists in order to obtain consent from local communities to install nuclear power. Indeed, such efforts contributed to the development of one of the strictest safety standards for nuclear power plants in the world. Simultaneously, however, the efforts helped to create a "safety myth" about nuclear power plants. In reality, it is not feasible to eliminate all risks in nuclear operations, even with the most rigorous and strict risk control and mitigation measures. Yet, even the existence of a minimal risk was not acceptable to the public, causing the government and power industry to demonstrate a situation of "zero-risk." This myth of complete and absolute safety gradually came to be perceived as a reality. Perpetuation of this myth led to the institutionalization of static and rigid nuclear safety measures.[14]

Risk of an accident at nuclear power plants can be reduced to zero only if all nuclear power plants are abandoned. Yet this will create another risk, growing vulnerability to external energy supply shocks or energy price fluctuations. Any discussion related to risk must not forget that there is always a tradeoff among different risks.[15] Increasing energy costs will further

14. Rebuild Japan Initiative Forum, *Fukushima Genpatsu Jiko Dokuritsu Kensho Iinkai Chousa Kenshou Houkokusho* [Research Report by Independent Investigation Commission of Fukushima Nuclear Power Plant Accident] (Discover 21, March 2012), 323–34.

15. Junko Nakanishi and Hiroko Kono, *Risuku to Mukiau* [Facing risks], Chuo Koronsha, 2012, 6–12. Toichi Tsutomu, *Shale Kakumei to Nihon no Enerugi* [Shale Revolution and Japan's Energy], Nihion Denki Kyokai Shimbunbu, October 2013, 192.

hurt the Japanese economy and thus affect the economic welfare and employment of the Japanese public. Ceasing all nuclear power generation also creates a serious security risk from the viewpoint of accumulating nuclear spent fuel in Japan. To address these issues properly, the dichotomous discussion of whether risk is zero or not needs to be replaced with a more objective discussion based on a probabilistic approach that accounts for tradeoffs. For example, the probability of a severe nuclear accident would be compared with the probability of severe economic impacts arising from a zero-nuclear option. Initiating this conversation may take a long time, but it is necessary for Japan's energy security and resilience.

Diversifying Supply Sources
Another important measure to mitigate the impacts of energy supply disruptions is diversification. Diversification of oil supply has been a long-standing goal for Japan's energy security policy. Geographical diversification of oil supply has to become a reality not only because oil still makes up the largest energy source for Japan but also because Japan's major supply sources are concentrated in the Middle East.[16] Japan continues to import Middle Eastern crude oil because it is economical; Japan can secure a lot of cargo by utilizing a very large crude carrier (VLCC). In fact, except for several extreme situations such as the Gulf War in 1991, oil flows from the Middle East have been quite stable and reliable.

Two favorable developments may aid in Japan's efforts to achieve geographical diversification. The first is the potential for crude oil exports from the United States. Thanks to the shale revolution, U.S. net oil imports in 2012 dropped by almost 40

16. Japan's dependence on Middle Eastern LNG imports (29.1 percent of total imports in 2012) is far smaller than its dependence on the region's oil (83.2 percent in 2012), but the share has been increasing steadily due to growth in demand caused by the shutdown of the nuclear power plants.

percent from their 2005 peak.[17] Crude oil supply in the United States has shifted from scarcity to abundance. The recent large discount of the U.S. benchmark crude oil price against the European benchmark shows this changing market reality.[18] Backed by such a rapid growth of production and the oil supply glut in the American Midwest, there is a vocal movement among U.S. lawmakers and policymakers, and in the U.S. oil industry, to review the existing export restrictions.[19] In addition to the import of crude oil produced from shale reservoirs, import of Alaskan oil is also a possibility. Japan imported Alaskan North Slope crude oil until the 1990s. The crude oil's quality is similar to the Middle Eastern crude oil that Japanese refiners are accustomed to processing. Alaska's geographic proximity to Japan further increases the attractiveness of this option. While it takes approximately 18 days to transport crude oil from the Gulf of Mexico to Japan, it takes only 12 days to go from Alaska to Japan. Existing export infrastructure in Alaska will also be a big cost saver and advantage if the state restarts exports of its

17. According to the U.S. Energy Information Administration (EIA), the net import volume of the United States in 2012 was 7.6 million b/d while its net import volume was 12.5 million b/d in 2005. EIA website: http://www.eia.gov/.

18. The U.S. benchmark crude price (West Texas Intermediate) had typically been higher than the European benchmark (Brent) by $1/barrel. But since 2011, the U.S. benchmark has been lower than the European by almost $10/barrel.

19. Senator Lisa Murkowski (R-AK), ranking member of the Senate Committee on Energy and Natural Resources, publicly claimed in January 2014 that the existing restriction is anarchic and should be ended. ("The Future of Energy Trade: A Conversation with Senator Lisa Murkowski," Brookings Institution, January 7, 2014.) In December 2013, Energy Secretary Ernest Moniz said that the United States needs to review the restriction established when oil supply was scarce. ("Energy Secretary Calls Oil Export Ban Dated," *New York Times*, December 13, 2013.) Some have suggested that the restriction of crude oil exports in the Unites States may violate the rules of the World Trade Organization (WTO). ("Oil Supply Surge Brings Calls to Ease U.S. Export Ban," Bloomberg, December 17, 2013.)

crude oil to Asia. If U.S. export restrictions are lifted, imports of Alaskan crude oil may be a more likely and realistic scenario for Japan than imports of shale oil.

Another favorable movement for diversifying Japan's crude oil supply is Russia's increasing interest in developing Siberian oil resources. Due to a stagnant economy, the maturing oil demand in Europe, and Russia's need to find another supply source to make up the depleting existing oil fields in Western Siberia, Russia has become more interested in developing its resources in the East.[20] Russia is already an established crude oil exporter in Asian markets, supplying more than one million barrels per day. The country has built pipelines toward its Pacific coast and it is expected that more western crude oil will be directed eastward through this expanded capacity. Japan can take advantage of this increasing Russian crude oil supply to Asian markets.

Changing oil market balances will lead to a more diversified crude oil supply for Asia. IEEJ has developed a scenario for possible changes in crude oil supply flows in 2030 compared to today, as shown in Figures 2a and 2b. In 2030, oil demand in developed economies will shrink while import demand in emerging economies will grow. In this scenario, the center of gravity of the international crude oil market will shift decisively to Asia. African crude oil suppliers will export more crude oil to Asian markets because the demand of their traditional customer, the United States, will decline with the growth of domestic production. This means that Asian economies will have more geographically dispersed options from which to choose their crude oil supply sources. This outcome will contribute to impact mitigation of potential supply disruptions. At the same time, the Middle East will continue to be the

---

20. For further details, see Shoichi Itoh, *Russia Looks East: Energy Markets and Geopolitics of Northeast Asia* (Washington, DC: CSIS, July 2011), https://csis.org/files/publication/110721_Itoh_RussiaLooksEast_Web.pdf.

lowest-cost oil producer in the world and its competitiveness in Asian markets will remain dominant. Additional crude oil from non-Middle Eastern sources may ease the thirst of Asian crude oil demand growth, but will not overtake the position of the Middle East.

Pursuing further diversification of LNG supply is also an important task for Japan to undertake. Although its sources of LNG are currently more geographically varied in comparison to its oil supply (Figure 3), it is expected that Japan's supply sources will concentrate around a more limited number of suppliers in the future, such as Qatar and Australia. As the domestic demand of traditional suppliers like Indonesia and Malaysia increases, their export volumes will diminish. Increasing LNG imports from North America will also be a great opportunity for Japan's diversification. Six projects have already obtained export permission from the U.S. Department of Energy.[21] LNG projects along the coast surrounding the Gulf of Mexico, Alaskan LNG and Canadian LNG will potentially be important sources of diversification for Japan. Emerging supply sources in the Eastern Mediterranean and in Eastern Africa are also candidates for future diversification.

---

21. The projects that have obtained permission are Sabine Pass (May 20, 2011), Freeport (May 17, 2013), Lake Charles (August 7, 2013), Cove Point (September 11, 2013), Freeport Expansion (November 15, 2013), and Cameron (February 11, 2014).

Figure 2a: Crude Oil Trade Flows, 2012

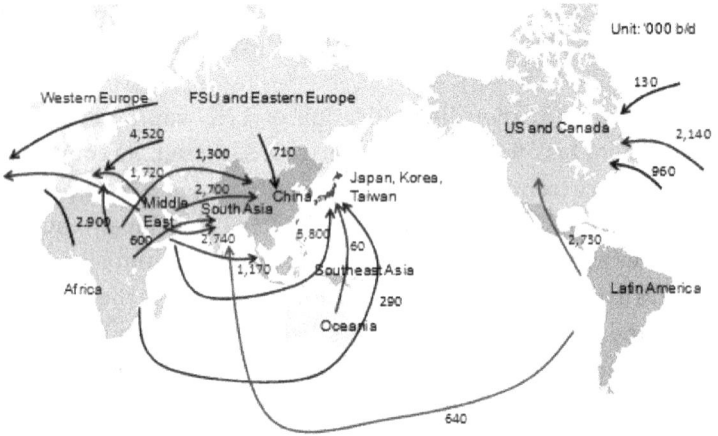

Source: Institute of Energy Economics, Japan.

Figure 2b: Crude Oil Trade Flows, 2030

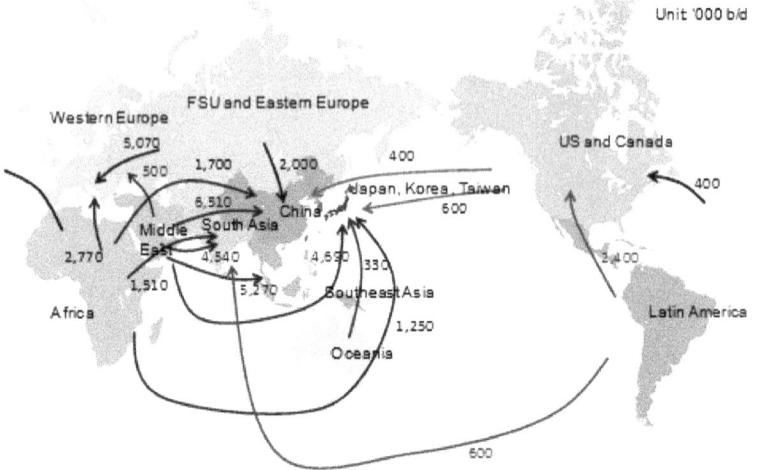

Source: Institute of Energy Economics, Japan.

Figure 3: LNG Import Sources of Japan, 2012

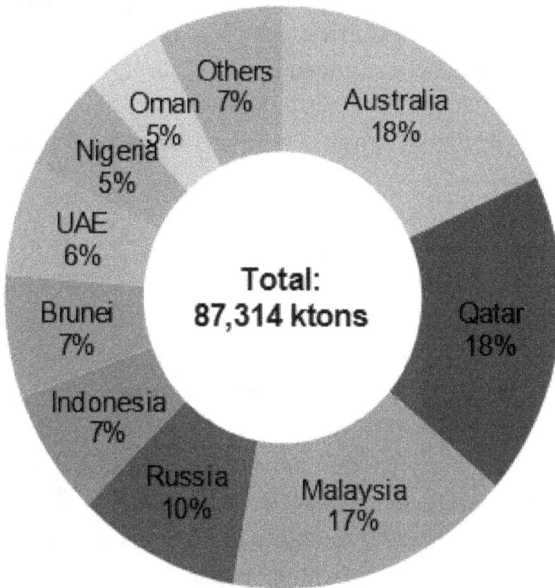

Source: Trade Statistics of Japan.

Diversifying Energy Pricing References

In addition to supply sources, it is important to diversify energy pricing references as well. In Japan, because most LNG supply prices are linked to the price of crude oil, more than 70 percent of Japan's energy supply is linked to a single energy price.[22] Linking natural gas prices to oil prices makes the Japanese economy more susceptible to volatile international oil markets. Traditionally, the Japanese LNG price has been linked to the average import price of crude oil in Japan because LNG was initially introduced as an alternative to oil in the power

---

22. The share is the sum of oil and natural gas over the total primary energy supply in fiscal year 2012. Energy Data and Modeling Center, Institute of Energy Economics, Japan.

generation sector. Forty years later, however, LNG no longer competes with oil in the power sector. Thus, linking LNG prices to oil prices has lost its historical justification. The existing pricing formula needs to be changed to more closely reflect the demand and supply balance of natural gas markets in order to enhance Japan's resilience when faced with oil price fluctuations.

Optimizing Thermal Power Generation Sources
Optimizing thermal power generation sources is equally important. Although renewable energy installation has proceeded quite rapidly in Japan, its share of total electricity generated is still negligible at 0.7 percent as of 2012.[23] It is therefore not realistic to assume renewable energy will be a majority share of Japan's energy supply in the short term. Thermal power generation must therefore play a substantial role. One energy policy specialist in Japan has argued that policy discussions of the electricity mix are weighted toward the debate over the utilization of nuclear energy and promotion of renewable energy sources. Little attention has been paid to thermal power generation, despite its supplying more than 90 percent of Japan's electricity needs.[24]

How to optimize the power generation mix needs to be discussed more comprehensively. LNG is undoubtedly a preferred fuel for power generation due to its lower carbon emissions and high heat efficiency if used in advanced technologies such as More Advanced Combined Cycle (MACC). Yet LNG cannot be stored in large quantities like crude oil because it evaporates

---

23. *Denki Jigyou Binran: Heisei 25 nendo-ban* [Bulletin on power industry 2013 edition], (Nihon Denki Kyoukai, November 2012). The figure excludes hydropower generation, which is 7.6 percent of total electricity generated in 2012.
24. Kikkawa Takeo, *Nihon-no Enerugi Mondai* [Japan's energy problem], (NTT Shuppan, November 2013), 9.

easily. Maintaining a certain share of coal- and oil-fired power generation in this regard is worth considering as a means of ensuring the resiliency of the power supply. The benefits of coal, namely its relatively low price compared with oil and gas and the political stability of its major suppliers, cannot be ignored even though its higher carbon content should be taken into account.

Oil, on the other hand, is a very flexible energy source, as it has a well-developed international market. In fact, oil-fired power generation has always played an important role when power demand surges in the summer time or if power supply capacity drops significantly, such as during the 3-11 earthquake. The market for oil for power generation is quite liquid and it is relatively easy to secure a required amount in a short period of time. This is a big difference from the LNG market, which is dominated by long-term contracts and is thus less flexible. Oil can also be stockpiled at a much lower cost than LNG and is less carbon intensive than coal. Although it is often ignored in energy policy discussions, the benefits of maintaining a certain share of oil in the power mix (from 5 percent to 10 percent) enhances high resilience and adaptability of the power supply system in case of emergency.

Taking Pragmatic Action on Climate Change
Finally, mitigation of potential damage caused by climate change is also an important item for Japan's energy policy. After the expiration of the Kyoto Protocol, the international community has failed to build an effective international framework to control greenhouse gas (GHGs) emissions. Slowdown in the economies of the world, particularly in Europe, has lowered attention to climate change issues. Emissions of GHGs, however, have continued to rise, and the risk of serious impacts caused by climate change has also increased. Japan, as a major

emitter of GHGs, should take the initiative to revive efforts to formulate and implement an international framework to respond to climate change, a very important task that will affect the welfare of future generations. The experiences of the Kyoto Protocol and successive negotiations in Conferences of the Parties (COP) meetings suggests that a "top-down" approach, or a process that identifies a global reduction target and then allocates numerical reduction targets to each country, will not obtain broader support, especially from emerging countries. The development of a more effective and realistic framework that emerging countries can ascend to more easily is needed. Such a framework should take a "bottom-up" approach where each country determines and commits to a carbon emissions reduction target that is not legally binding, and institutes a regular review process for following through on those pledges. This framework may sound too loose, but it is an important step to forging a global consensus to reduce carbon emissions. Japan could contribute to reducing global carbon emissions through transfer of technologies to developing economies. For instance, a bilateral carbon credit framework will further facilitate such technology transfer.

Guarding Free and Open Energy Market Transactions
Improving emergency response measures is another crucial pillar of enhancing resilience. Though Japan has traditionally paid less attention to this aspect, the most important precondition to a prompt recovery in the case of an unexpected supply disruption is a properly functioning international market. For a country like Japan that depends on imports for most of its energy supply, a free and open international market is necessary for its survival; barriers and restrictions to the free flow of energy supply should be minimized. We can expect Japan to continue to emphasize the virtue of free and open interna-

tional markets in various forums. The subject should always be on the agenda at international organizations like the International Energy Agency, and other multinational frameworks such as the Asia-Pacific Economic Cooperation (APEC), Association of Southeast Asian Nations+3 (ASEAN+3), G-8, and G-20. Multilateral trade frameworks such as the Trans-Pacific Partnership (TPP) should also include provisions for free trade in the international energy market.

Recent examples in which free and open markets contributed to prompt recovery from oil supply disruption include those caused by Hurricanes Katrina and Rita in August and September 2005. After hitting the southern part of the United States, these hurricanes seriously damaged both oil producing facilities and refineries. The oil supply was restricted in both the northern and southern United States as hurricanes damaged power supplies required to operate oil pipelines connecting refining centers along the coast of the Gulf of Mexico and the northern United States. Domestic gasoline futures rose sharply before the hurricanes but despite the extent of the damage the price soon fell back to pre-hurricane levels of around $2.00 per gallon in just 10 days.[25] The U.S. government's swift decision to release its Strategic Petroleum Reserves, as well as the collective release of oil stockpiles by International Energy Agency member countries, undoubtedly helped to ease concerns about a supply shortage in the market. Yet the most decisive force was price signaling. Loss of oil production and refining capacity raised domestic energy prices significantly and the high price relative to international levels attracted product imports from all over the world.[26] No other system rivals free-market mechanisms for allocating limited resources optimally. To this end,

---

25. EIA website: http://www.eia.gov/dnav/pet/pet_pri_gnd_dcus_nus_w.htm.
26. U.S. gasoline imports from August 2005 to December 2005 increased by 28 percent from 138 million barrels to 177 million barrels. EIA website: http://www.eia.gov/dnav/pet/pet_move_impcus_a2_nus_epobg_imo_mbbl_m.htm.

guarding the current international liquid oil and coal market as well as improving liquidity in international LNG markets is the highest priority for Japan's emergency response system.[27]

Guaranteeing Free and Open International Maritime Order
Free and open maritime order based on the international rule of law is a fundamental premise of market utilization in the case of an emergency. Japan has to work to ensure such an environment is in place in case of unexpected supply risks.[28] Since geopolitical tensions along the sea lines of communication (SLOCs) from the Strait of Hormuz to the South China Sea and East China Sea have been heightened, preserving maritime order has become far more important than in the past. Japan's past energy security discussions have not focused on these maritime security issues. Given the increasing geopolitical tensions over the SLOCs, however, guarding a free and open maritime order has to be regarded as a primary policy goal for energy resilience efforts.

Solidifying the alliance with the United States is a cornerstone of ensuring a free and open maritime order, as is security cooperation with like-minded countries such as Korea, Australia, and India. Above all, cooperation with ASEAN countries will become a priority for Japan because they are located along SLOCs and Japan shares common interests with these countries. Most ASEAN countries are energy importers. Coopera-

27. Many of the past oil supply disruptions besides Hurricanes Katrina and Rita were resolved essentially by the market function and price signal. See Eugene Gholz and Daryl G. Press, "Protecting 'The Prize': Oil and the U.S. National Interest," *Security Studies* 19 (2010): 453–85.
28. The significance of and measures to ensure free and open maritime order for Japanese energy supply are discussed in detail in Rebuild Japan Initiative Foundation's Japan-US Strategic Vision Program, "'Shizuka na Yokushiryoku' wo Kouchiku Suru: Pawa Tagenka Jidai no 'Senryakuteki Kokueki'" [Building 'Quiet Deterrence': 'Strategic national interest' in the age of multiple powers], *Chuo-Koron* (January 2014), 146–56.

tion with ASEAN countries could include technical assistance for coast guard services and sharing of navigation safety information. Japan could also encourage ASEAN to solidify their actions to ensure a maritime order based on international rule of law.

The relationship with China is critically important for Japan's security and economic prosperity, and thus Japan should continue dialogue with China to encourage China to view a free and open maritime order as beneficial. Since China's recent naval activities are to some extent driven by the need to secure its energy supply, Japan is ready to cooperate with China to ease its energy security concerns. Japan can do so by sharing its expertise on stockpiling developments and operations, its experiences recovering from natural disasters, and its expertise with energy conservation to alleviate concerns regarding unexpected energy supply disruptions.

Developing Prompt and Adaptive Government Decisionmaking
Prompt decisionmaking is required in emergencies. The allocation of limited resources such as food, medical supplies, and energy products requires a prioritization philosophy or guidelines. In the case of the 3-11 earthquake and tsunami, for instance, oil product supply to the quake-hit area was coordinated through close communication between the Agency of Natural Resource and Energy and the oil industry. But this arrangement was not determined a priori; rather, it was established in a muddle-through process after the disaster. Supply arrangements were made on an ad hoc basis. In hindsight, due to interruptions in communication, there was not adequate information on supply requirements and distribution was not carried out in a well-organized manner. Predetermined processes to establish such supply coordination mechanisms, as well as to prioritize supply to one location or purpose over

another for limited supply resources, will facilitate prompt recovery in case of emergency.

Furthermore, the introduction of adaptive and flexible regulatory arrangements may be important in order to facilitate a prompt recovery. During the 3-11 earthquake, several regulations became a barrier toward rapid recovery. In the case of the oil supply, donated oil products from China could not be discharged immediately because quality specifications for products were slightly different from those of Japan. Additionally, tanker trucks could not drive through long-distance tunnels for safety reasons and were unable to supply oil products to quake-hit areas. The fact that coastal tanker regulations require Japanese-flagged vessels to be used to transport cargo between Japanese ports may also prove a large obstacle when stockpiled oil is released to refineries. These regulations are of course meaningful for safety, environmental, and security purposes. In case of an emergency, however, they should be relaxed for a predetermined, short period of time to ensure prompt recovery. Identifying priority areas for temporary relaxation and determining a procedure to enact such relaxation requires attention.

Implementing Nationwide and Interagency Exercises
As a further step toward solidifying the government's capabilities, nationwide exercises should be undertaken. Such exercises should be conducted with all related organizations from the Cabinet Office to the Ministry of Economy, Trade, and Industry; the Ministry of Land, Infrastructure, and Transportation; the National Police Agency; the Fire and Disaster Management Agency; and the Ministry of Defense. Nationwide emergency response exercises in fact have been conducted for potential nuclear power plant accidents in accordance with the Disaster Countermeasures Basic Act and the Act on Special Measures

Concerning Nuclear Emergency Preparedness. The scope of such an exercise could be expanded to include nonnuclear energy supply as well and various potential scenarios such as severe natural disasters or disruption of energy imports. Private companies that play an important role in the operation of vital public goods and services such as energy companies and public transportation companies could be invited to join the exercise. The proper functioning of the response system requires that Japan identify potential problems in decisionmaking, information collection, and analysis; communicate among ministries and agencies; demarcate the roles and the mission of government and industry; and conduct nationwide exercises.

Mobilizing Stockpiles

Stockpiling is a classic measure of energy security. As mentioned above, Japan holds more than 180 days consumption equivalent for crude oil stockpiles, which is among the largest of the Organization for Economic Cooperation and Development (OECD) countries. In order to enhance Japan's energy resilience, Japan could improve the "mobilization" of the current energy stockpile. In other words, crude oil stored in a stockpile would not just remain in a storage tank but would flow continuously while maintaining the total level of inventory. Enhancing mobility of stockpiling would facilitate prompt release when it is needed, and also, by rotating the stockpiled crude oil, the grade of crude oil could be replaced to meet changing grade preferences of domestic refiners. Japanese oil stockpiles, especially government stockpiles, have been static and seldom released so far; but it would be preferable to transform this static stockpile into one that is more mobile and dynamically utilized.

There are several policy developments in this regard. The Japanese government introduced a joint stockpiling arrangement with major Middle Eastern oil suppliers such as the United Arab Emirates in 2009 and Saudi Arabia in 2011. This is a framework that allows oil producers to use Japanese stockpiling facilities for storage, while in exchange Japan gains priority access in case of an emergency. By allowing oil-producing countries to use stockpiling facilities, stored oil continues to be sold and replenished and promotes a shift in stockpiled oil from staying oil to flowing oil. Another attempt to make Japanese stockpiling more dynamic is to expand oil product stockpiling for commercial purposes. This expansion was introduced in 2012 after the 2011 earthquake where 30 percent of domestic refining capacity was lost in the immediate aftermath. Because stockpiled oil products have to be replaced regularly, unlike crude oil stockpiling, to avoid quality degradation, this will also "mobilize" stockpiled oil in Japan.

A further step worth considering to promote this flowing stockpile would be regular test releases. These releases could be done as part of the government-wide emergency exercise discussed above. The procedure for such a release needs to be elaborated upon, and the current regulation requiring that Japanese-flagged tanker vessels transport crude oil between Japanese ports may require review. Due to Japan's dependence on oil supply imports, effective operation of stockpiles will be crucial to its emergency response planning efforts.

How to Balance Economic Competitiveness?
The actions mentioned above for enhancing energy resilience are not free. Some measures require additional expenditures while others demand infrastructure redundancy. In Japan, most energy supplies are undertaken and maintained by private companies and it is not realistic to have only these players

undertake actions that enhance Japan's ability to recover from a crisis. Actions that private business cannot undertake should certainly be in the domain of the government.

It should be noted at the same time, however, that resilience enhancement is often paired with commercial benefit for private players. Given the potential for significant impact from an emergency, limited additional expenditures to enhance resilience should be regarded as an insurance premium that will reasonably reduce future uncertainties in business activities. Strengthening capabilities for impact mitigation and prompt recovery from damage incurred is also considered a matter of competitiveness for an economy or firm. Diversification is sometimes associated with logistical or quality risks if an unfamiliar energy cargo is acquired. But at the same time, if pursued properly it will give more leverage to the buyer against seller.

Any action toward greater resilience must not be static, of course. Actions have to be reviewed to determine whether costs associated with any action are justified through defended wealth or avoided expenditures. Striking the best balance will remain a central interest in resilience enhancement.

U.S.-JAPAN ENERGY COOPERATION: SETTING-UP OF STRATEGIC ENERGY DIALOGUE

The U.S.-Japan alliance, needless to say, plays a crucial role in enhancing Japan's energy resilience. First of all, LNG exports from the United States will further solidify our bilateral relationships because, as already mentioned, it has significant effects on Japan's diversification of supply sources and energy prices. If all of the proposed LNG export projects that plan to export to Japan (Freeport, Cove Point, and Cameron) were realized, 17 million tons of LNG would be exported to Japan. The volume exceeds the export from Qatar to Japan in 2013 and ranks second only after Australia of total Japanese LNG imports in 2013. This level of exports will certainly have a material impact to Japan's diversification effort as well as Asia's LNG market balance.

Even though not all of these projects would start up as scheduled, U.S. LNG exports to Japan will have a symbolic meaning for the alliance. No doubt there is an economic motivation to export LNG to capture the rents caused by the natural price difference in the U.S. and Asian market. As the study commissioned by the Department of Energy reveals, LNG exports will bring net benefits to the U.S. economy on a macro basis.[29] The export of energy, however, always has a different political sensitivity as energy is a critical resource for all economies. The U.S. manufacturing and petrochemical industries repeatedly argue against the U.S. government's pro-export attitude.[30] There remains concern of potential price spikes in the natural gas market as actually observed when the United States was hit by very cold weather in February 2014. U.S. willingness to export LNG to non-free trade agreement (FTA) countries like Japan, despite all these concerns and opposition within the United States, is interpreted as a sign of U.S. intention to assist with the restoration of the post-earthquake Japanese economy. Increased trade of a vital commodity such as LNG will naturally draw U.S. attention to free and safe maritime order to the Asia-Pacific basin. This will accelerate the U.S. rebalancing policy to Asia and will have a favorable effect on the U.S.-Japan alliance.

LNG export, though it has significant meaning for Japan and

29. NERA Economic Consulting, *Macroeconomic Impacts of LNG Exports from the United States* (Washington, DC: NERA Economic Consulting, December 2012), http://energy.gov/sites/prod/files/2013/04/f0/nera_lng_report.pdf.

30. Companies such as Alcoa and Dow Chemical are opposing LNG exports because of concerns about the rise of natural gas prices due to increased exports. For details, see the website of America's Energy Advantage, an organization founded by these companies, at http://www.americasenergyadvantage.org/.

the United States, is only a part of bilateral energy cooperation. Another equally important area for the bilateral cooperation is nuclear energy. Japan and the United States have developed cooperative partnerships in civil utilization of nuclear energy since the 1950s, and have deepened cooperation since the current Japan-U.S. Nuclear Power Cooperation Agreement went into effect in 1988. The earthquake in 2011 provided additional momentum to the bilateral nuclear energy cooperation. President Obama and then-prime minister Noda agreed to the U.S.-Japan Bilateral Commission on Civil Nuclear Cooperation in April 2012. The commission intends to "facilitate discussions on future nuclear energy cooperation; and advance shared interests in nuclear safety and security, nonproliferation, counterterrorism, decommissioning and decontamination, emergency preparedness and response, and research and development."[31] In February 2004, the two countries held a working group meeting to discuss the advancement and adoption of Probabilistic Risk Assessment methodology for nuclear power plants' operation.[32] The next step is, in accordance with the agreement of the bilateral commission, to expand the scope of cooperation to areas such as nuclear security and emergency response.

Nuclear energy, despite the severe accident at Fukushima, has gained further importance due to growing energy demand in the developing world, the increasing need to reduce global greenhouse gas emissions, and chronic geopolitical uncertainties in major oil and gas producing regions. Sharing its experi-

31. Ministry of Foreign Affairs of Japan, "Summary results of the US-Japan bilateral committee first meeting on civilian nuclear cooperation," press release, July 24, 2012, http://www.mofa.go.jp/mofaj/press/release/24/7/0724_04.html.

32. Ministry of Economy, Trade, and Industry of Japan, "'Probabilistic risk assessment US-Japan Round Table' improve safety of nuclear power," press release, February 14, 2014, http://www.meti.go.jp/press/2013/02/20140214003/20140214003.html.

ence of long-term peaceful use of nuclear energy and lessons from the Fukushima Daiichi accident with all existing and future nuclear energy users is Japan's global responsibility. As leading countries in civil nuclear energy, the United States and Japan have to tighten their collaborative relations to ensure safe and peaceful expansion of nuclear energy in the world.

In light of the increasing importance of energy between the two countries, establishing a bilateral strategic energy dialogue is worth considering. Its primarily private companies both in Japan and the United States that undertake the energy market and business activities, and government intervention has to be minimized. Yet regulatory issues such as LNG exports or, in the long term, crude oil exports as well as nuclear security and safety issues cannot be discussed and promoted without serious commitments by both governments. Regular meetings at the minister level will accelerate the development of bilateral cooperation and solidify the U.S.-Japan alliance.

CONCLUSION

Tabel 2 summarizes the preceding discussion. Resilience aims to make the Japanese energy supply system more adaptive and responsive to supply shocks.

Uncertainties in international energy markets have been increasing. The experience of the 3-11 earthquake has provided lessons for Japan. All these factors and lessons have to be reflected in Japan's energy security policy, and enhancing energy resilience is one of the directions that Japan should pursue. Some measures mentioned above may be relatively easy to undertake, while others may take a long time. Japan does not have the luxury to defer its efforts from greater energy resilience. Since the experience and memory of the earthquake is still fresh among the Japanese public and a new Basic Energy

Plan has been published, now is the right time for the Japanese government and public to discuss and act to enhance resilience in Japan's energy supply. ▪

Table 2: Elements of Japan's Traditional Energy Security and Energy Resilience

	Traditional energy security	Energy resilience
Primary policy goal	Risk prevention and impact mitigation.	Impact mitigation and emergency response.
Diversification	Significant efforts have been made but the supply of oil is still concentrated in the Middle East.	New supply potential has emerged and may ease Japan's high dependence on the Middle East.
Perceived energy supply disruption	Geopolitical events in energy-producing countries.	Whole supply chain including safe navigation to Japan and domestic energy supply.
Views about energy supply risk	Risk can be minimized through rigorous mitigation measures.	Risk cannot be fully removed. Risk needs to be managed based on probabilistic approach considering risk tradeoffs.
Stockpiling operation	Static stockpile.	Mobilized stockpile.
Regulatory actions in case of emergency	Static.	Adaptive and flexible.

Source: Author.

6. JAPAN'S STRATEGY TOWARD SOUTHEAST ASIA AND THE JAPAN-U.S. ALLIANCE

Nobuhiro Aizawa[1]

BACKGROUND

Southeast Asia, with a population of more than 620 million and a growing working-age middle class, is beginning to reap the benefits of its demographic dividend. Southeast Asia's total gross domestic product (GDP) was $2.3 trillion in 2012, bigger than India's and 12.5 percent of the total GDP of Asia, making it one of the largest and fastest-growing markets in the world. The development of supply chain linkages in the region has increased intraregional interdependence in Southeast Asia and multilateral free trade agreements (FTAs) have also helped to connect it to other parts of the world.

Southeast Asia occupies a critical strategic geopolitical location in the Asia-Pacific's maritime and aviation networks. It

1. I would like to express my deepest gratitude especially to all my colleagues at CSIS, in particular Michael Green, Ernie Bower, Victor Cha, Nicholas Szechnyi, and Zack Cooper for the wonderful feedback and for their wholehearted support in writing this paper. Also, I would like to thank Satu Limaye from the East-West Center, Thomas Vallely and Benny Subianto from Harvard University, Ginandjar Kartasasmita from the Indonesia Presidential Advisory Board, Toshihiro Kudo from the Institute of Developing Economies-Japan External Trade Organization (IDE-JETRO), and Takashi Shiraishi from the Graduate Research Institute for Policy Studies (GRIPS) Japan for all their inputs. Needless to say, any errors and misunderstandings are mine.

lies at the crossroads of the Pacific Ocean and the Indian Ocean and astride key global sea lanes and chokepoints, such as the Malacca Strait and the South China Sea. Each year $5.3 trillion worth of shipping passes through the waterways of Southeast Asia.[2] In addition, Bangkok and Singapore function as key hub airports connecting passengers traveling to and from Oceania, Northeast Asia, and South Asia. In terms of international passenger traffic in 2013, Singapore and Bangkok rank numbers five and eight in the world, respectively.[3] A well-connected Asia-Pacific, or Indo-Pacific, is not possible without an open and active Southeast Asia.

In this era of economic integration, Southeast Asian countries have chosen to diversify internationally to maximize their security and stability. This focus on diversification, or "risk hedging," seeks to avoid assertive action by non-Southeast Asian countries, including China, Japan, or the United States. Southeast Asia's priority is keeping diversification feasible. In addition to Southeast Asia's growing economic power, it also has gained substantial diplomatic influence through collective decisionmaking in the Association of Southeast Asian Nations (ASEAN), East Asia Summit (EAS), and Asia-Pacific Economic Cooperation (APEC), as well as ASEAN+3 and ASEAN+6 meetings.

In 2013, Japan made clear Southeast Asia's strategic importance when Prime Minister Shinzo Abe visited 10 Southeast Asian countries in a single year, a first not only for a Japanese prime minister, but for all non-ASEAN leaders. This ASEAN-focused diplomacy culminated in the ASEAN-Japan Com-

---

2. ASEAN Matters for America/America Matters for ASEAN, East West Center, Washington, DC, http://www. asiamattersforamerica.org/sites/all/themes/eastwestcenter/pdfs/Asean_Matters_for_America_bro-chure2.pdf.
3. Airports Council International's 2013 data, http://www.aci.aero/Data-Centre/Annual-Traffic-Data.

memorative Summit in December 2013, in which Japan and ASEAN released a joint statement announcing: "We recognized the important role that ASEAN and Japan could play to address regional and global challenges and exchanged our views on issues of common interests."[4]

JAPAN'S STRATEGIC GOAL

Japan's first regional goal should be to build a stronger Southeast Asia. This strategic goal is important for two reasons. First, it is crucial that Southeast Asia be a stable and prosperous region for its own wellbeing. Second, a stronger Southeast Asia would make Asia as a whole more balanced, stable, and prosperous. A unipolar Asia would create space for power-based intraregional politics. To make Asia stable and prosperous and to encourage a rules/consensus-based Asia—a balanced multipolar Asia (e.g., China, India, ASEAN, and Japan)—is important. Southeast Asia, as the region where we can expect accelerated growth while China's growth slows, will hold vital strategic meaning and determine whether Asia can be stabilized as a whole.

Japan's second goal should be to reinforce its status as Southeast Asia's legitimate partner. In other words, Japan needs to gain legitimacy by leading and being endorsed by its partners and neighbors. Strength is a prerequisite, but legitimacy is critical considering the destructive power of modern weaponry and Asia's closely interconnected economy. The competition today is not simply over power itself, but a more subtle competition for legitimacy, which defines the way states use their accumulated power.

Japan's third goal relates to the classic phrase: "Foreign policy begins at home." Japan's strategy is best accomplished by

---

4. "Hand in hand, facing regional and global challenges," Joint Statement of the ASEAN-Japan Commemorative Summit, December 14, 2013, http://www.mofa.go.jp/mofaj/files/000022451.pdf.

satisfying domestic needs, which is why Southeast Asia is likely to matter more as Japan faces the demographic challenges of an aging society. Japan will need a stable and active partnership with an emerging community of great talent and youth. Japan is one of the few countries that has enjoyed a long-term, stable, strong, and peaceful relationship with Southeast Asian countries for more than 40 years. There is no place like Southeast Asia that has shared stable relations with Japan, and becoming its closest partner is strategically important for Japan's prosperity in the decades to come.

Japan's fourth goal acknowledges that as it is neither the economic giant it was 30 years ago, nor a military powerhouse, it is crucial to redefine Japan's role in Southeast Asia and the broader global society. Japan's national strength is best described by the term "resiliency." Japan has demonstrated its resilience in terms of economic and disaster relief policies, but resilience could also be valuable in Japan's diplomacy. Japan's diplomacy should seek to build a "resilient society" in Southeast Asia and the broader region. This policy is a good fit because it is also a goal in Southeast Asia. In 2013, at the APEC meeting in Bali, Indonesia, APEC leaders led by President Susilo Bambang Yudhoyono of Indonesia called for a "resilient Asia-Pacific, engine of global growth." This is a golden moment for Japan to match its values with those of ASEAN.

ENHANCING RESILIENCY IN SOUTHEAST ASIA

In pursuit of these goals, Japan's strategy for strengthening Southeast Asia should be to enhance "four resiliencies" in Southeast Asia: economic, political, environmental, and security.

Economic Resilience

Keeping Southeast Asian production capability strong and maintaining connectivity among both markets and networks is a shared Southeast Asian, Japanese, American, and even Chinese interest. The sustainability or resilience of the current liberal economic order is yet to be confirmed. High-performing economies in the region—such as Indonesia, Thailand, Malaysia, the Philippines, and Singapore—aspire to attain the next level of development, following in the footsteps of Taiwan and South Korea. However, their economic resilience needs to be enhanced to address challenges to Southeast Asia's economies, such as economic disparities.

The strength of Southeast Asia's economy in the coming decades is no longer just low-cost labor or natural resources—it is the growing middle class. Japan now has more invested in Southeast Asia than in China, which had been Japan's favorite investment target.[5] Southeast Asia is not only a production engine, but a rapidly growing consumption engine as well. To maintain stable, sustainable, and balanced growth is particularly important for major economic partners, such as Japan, the United States, and China.

The Southeast Asian consumer market is highly attractive to Japanese businesses given the shrinking size of Japan's own population and its aging society. Due to Japan's demographic constraints, its companies inevitably go abroad and invest for growth and survival. Ultimately, Japan's objective is to establish a middle class that shares

5. In the first half of 2013, Japanese foreign direct investment (FDI) in Southeast Asia reached $10.3 billion (a 50 percent increase compared with 2012)—more than twice its FDI in China, which stood at $5 billion (a 30 percent decrease compared with 2012). In the first half of 2009, FDI in Southeast Asia and China were roughly equal, at around $7 billion. Since then, Japanese FDI in Southeast Asia has surpassed that in China. The exception is 2012, when Thailand suffered a particularly serious flood that damaged the country's key industrial zones. (See *Nikkei Shimbun*, November 20, 2013). Also, the Japanese automobile industry sold 2.73 million new cars in ASEAN in 2012, equivalent to its sales in China for that year. Its market share in Southeast Asia was 79 percent, but dropped to 20 percent in China in the wake of the crisis over the Senkaku Islands. See *Nikkei Shimbun*, September 11, 2013.

Japanese values and a secure, open, and connected Southeast Asia.

The major challenge for Southeast Asia to enhancing its economic resiliency is decreasing two economic disparities. The first challenge is domestic disparity. Poverty remains a serious concern and the income gap is widening in each country. Geographical distribution of wealth within countries is highly unbalanced, as major metropolitan areas take a larger share of growth while peripheries are left underdeveloped. The second challenge is intraregional disparity among Southeast Asian countries, which could be a major destabilizing factor for Southeast Asia. This is particularly problematic in Cambodia, Laos, and Myanmar (the CLM countries) as well as other ASEAN member states. As the ASEAN Economic Community seeks economic integration by the end of 2015, ASEAN depends more and more on private corporations' supply chain management. Thus, the character of economic competition in ASEAN will be a contest for high-value-added components of the supply chain. In this regard, there is a "first mover advantage" or a "lock-in effect" that favors countries such as Thailand, Malaysia, Singapore, Indonesia, and now Vietnam. The CLM countries need to catch up in order to avoid being trapped in low-value-added economic areas, as demonstrated by the "smiling curve" model. This structural unfairness could lead to dissention within Southeast Asia, which could potentially spill over to security issues.

Political Resilience
In recent years Indonesia, Japan, the United States, and others have helped Myanmar gain international trust and respect, particularly in Southeast Asia. President Thein Sein, despite being a high-ranking military general during Tan Shwe's regime, has achieved credibility in committing himself to major political

reforms. However, it is too early to be assured of Myanmar's long-term political stability. Various challenges lie ahead, such as constitutional privileges for the military, prohibitions preventing Aung San Suu Kyi from running for president, and the lack of protections for ethnic minorities.[6]

The major question for Southeast Asia's political stability, especially in democratic countries, is how election losers accept defeat. Democratization does not guarantee economic development, stable commodity prices, higher wages, or ousting the old elite. Defeated politicians too often reject their defeat, as in Thailand, which is a danger to Myanmar and Cambodia as well. In all of these countries, especially in the current era when a military coup is a costly choice, the key institution for political stability is the judicial system, which has played a critical role in Thailand and set the stage for the coup d'etat in 2014.[7]

Japan and the United States can support maintaining political stability in Southeast Asia by promoting liberal democracy (i.e., free and fair elections, accountability, free media access, respect for human rights, and prohibition of xenophobic policies). Interethnic and intermigrant social structures and his-

---

6. Whether people will accept the election result in 2015 if Aung San Suu Kyi is not allowed to run for president remains an open question. Questions also remain about whether the National League for Democracy (NLD) can gain trust from minorities and manage ethnic conflicts, particularly with Muslims in Rakhine.

7. The role of judicial power is gaining importance as politics of the middle-income trap creates a platform for politicians to leverage their influence by capitalizing on feelings of economic nationalism. As we saw in the political battle not only in Thailand but also in Indonesia over the 2009 New Mineral Law and the Indonesian Constitutional Court's 2012 ruling dissolving BP Migas, it is now the judicial institutions that play a critical role to manage politicized economic issues as well. Labor movements and their demands for welfare in countries that manufacture or produce goods will be a hot-button issue. Japanese companies must have comprehensive knowledge of these dynamics, especially in the coming five years. It is vital that Japan understand how Southeast Asian governments will handle these new demands.

torical legacies are landmines that could derail democracy and economic growth in the region. The United States and Japan must work together to prevent ethnic issues from setting back democratic reforms.

Environmental Resilience
The main threats to human life in Southeast Asia have been environmental disasters, such as typhoons in the Philippines, floods in Bangkok, and volcanic eruptions and earthquakes in Indonesia. Disaster relief, therefore, is a key pillar of good governance. The challenge for Southeast Asian countries is to enhance disaster management capability, in order to secure the lives and livelihood of their nations, promote environmentally safe and energy-efficient economic development, and build urban infrastructures in densely populated Southeast Asia.

This is an area in which Japan can make a major difference. Japan's experience in handling natural disasters, such as the 2013 Tohoku Great Earthquake and the tsunami, demonstrates its capacity for both civil and military cooperation. Multinational humanitarian assistance/disaster relief (HA/DR) operations in the Philippines were a huge step forward in establishing a more resilient Asia. This practice should be cemented as a new area of cooperation in Asia to address the common threat of natural disasters.

Security Resilience
To maintain Southeast Asia as an open and stable economy, resilience in the field of security is indispensable, especially given the changing power balance in the region. Enhancing Southeast Asian security serves not only the respective countries in Southeast Asia, but also the whole of Asia. One key norm is the maintenance of freedom of navigation through strategically important sea-lanes (the Malacca Strait, South China Sea,

and East China Sea) and freedom of overflight.[8] Securing these global commons is vital to ensuring the region's continued economic growth and the smooth exchange of goods, information, and people.

The Philippines and Vietnam (and to a lesser degree Malaysia and Brunei) are facing maritime challenges from China in the South China Sea. This is a major threat not only to the sovereign claims of these countries, but also to every state whose economic activity is connected to the South China Sea. Asia's vibrant economy relies heavily on freedom of navigation in the South China Sea. For example, approximately 95 percent of Japan's energy supplies and 40 percent of its maritime trade passes through the South China Sea. Thus, maritime security in the South China Sea is critical to Japanese national interests. With China now projecting power throughout the South China Sea and challenging Southeast Asian countries, the way this dispute is solved will be crucial to the security of the region as a whole.

Three challenges complicate the South China Sea case. First, there is a clear asymmetric power relationship between the Southeast Asian countries and China. Southeast Asia's maritime law-enforcement capacity is limited compared to China's. This asymmetric power relationship offers little chance for Southeast Asian countries to establish their claims or to settle upon a code of conduct. Instead, China has been using its advantages to prolong the process, pursuing fait accompli actions to cement a "new status quo" in negotiations.

For Southeast Asian countries facing this impasse, choices are limited. The first option is to stand up to China and main-

---

8. The phrase "free and safe maritime navigation and aviation" was coined at the ASEAN-Japan Summit in December 2013 and was a major topic of consensus building. See http://www.mofa.go.jp/files/000022451.pdf.

tain the principle of reciprocity. However, the lesson from the standoff over Scarborough Shoal and other reefs and islands is that the costs proved too big to handle bilaterally.[9] Since the 2010 crisis between Japan and China, neighboring countries have also learned that China can utilize trade as a weapon in its bid to force policy changes in countries with which it has international disputes. Thus, only a few big countries such as the United States, India, and Japan can choose this option in disputes.

The second option is to counterbalance China by cooperating with another major power (i.e., the United States). This strategy is favored by the Philippines and Vietnam, which have appealed to the United States to support their claims.[10] The difficulty for Southeast Asian countries in choosing this strategy is the possibility of being forced to "take sides" with either China or the United States. Being forced to "take sides" was precisely the dilemma that Cambodia confronted during its chairmanship of ASEAN; international pressure was aimed at Cambodia, which Cambodia absolutely wanted to avoid.[11]

A third choice is to count on and to strengthen international laws and norms. Strengthening enforcement of international norms under the United Nations Convention on the Law of the Sea (UNCLOS) is a vital diplomatic channel. Using this approach, Japan can clearly demonstrate its common interests

---

9. China banned Filipino banana imports to "sanction" the latter nation during the Scarborough Shoal standoff. However, China denies this claim, saying it was a quarantine issue. Additionally, Chinese authorities restricted the issuance of tourist packages to the Philippines.
10. Secretary of State John Kerry was in Vietnam on December 14–16 and the Philippines on December 17–18, pledging the United States' commitment on maritime security assistance.
11. For Prime Minister Hun Sen, the toughest dilemma will be taking sides either with Vietnam or China rather than the United States or China, due to his personal political career. His ascendancy to power could not have happened without support from Vietnam.

and strategy with other littoral states in Southeast Asia. Therefore, Japan's strategy in this regard is to pursue multilateral and legal approaches by claiming that the situation is a common challenge to the global commons. With the first choice infeasible and the second choice forcing ASEAN to take sides, the third choice best serves ASEAN littoral states' interests.

The second challenge to enhancing Southeast Asian security is the ASEAN member states' different stances toward China. ASEAN can be effective only when the member nations have a consensus. Attitudes toward China naturally differ between countries depending on their geostrategic location, economic ties, and historical relationships. Despite the knowledge that bilateral negotiations disadvantage Southeast Asian countries, collective action has been difficult to coordinate. However, this does not mean that the ASEAN framework is ineffective. As Japan's strategy is to enhance ASEAN's collective position, cooperation in other areas could be important. For example, information sharing and capacity building through the ASEAN Regional Forum (ARF) and the Expanded ASEAN Maritime Forum could address nontraditional security issues such as piracy and disaster management in maritime zones. Activities such as the ASEAN Defense Ministers' Meeting Plus (ADMM-Plus) Humanitarian Assistance and Disaster Relief and Military Medicine Exercise held in Brunei in June 2013 have established cooperation among the defense forces of the ADMM-Plus countries under ASEAN.[12] Under this umbrella, ASEAN and Japan can enhance capacity and cooperation and can establish a framework that applies to gray-zone security challenges. Using the ASEAN-centered regional framework for nontra-

---

12. See Joint Declaration on the Second ASEAN Defence Ministers' Meeting Plus, Bandar Seri Begawan, August 29, 2013, http://www.mindef.gov.sg/imindef/press_room/official_releases/nr/2013/aug/29aug13_nr/29aug13_fs.html#. UoWepVdTDLU.

ditional security issues offers Japan an opportunity since this platform allows Japan and ASEAN states together with other key partners such as the United States, China, Korea, and Australia to address shared regional challenges together.

The third important challenge is that despite the security threats noted above, China remains an important partner and neighbor. Neither Japan nor its Southeast Asian friends can afford an all-out confrontational relationship with China. Both Southeast Asia and Japan need to be clear that there is no intention to contain China. Security resilience in the region is fundamentally about whether the rule of law can prevail over rule of power. If rule of power wins, the stability and prosperity of this region would cease. It is in the interest of ASEAN countries, Japan, the United States, and China that these nations secure an open ASEAN and keep Southeast Asia a place where law rules rather than power.

Taking the above three challenges into account, Southeast Asia can first enhance its security resilience by improving surveillance in maritime zones. The surveillance system is crucial because it is a prerequisite for effective law enforcement and settling disputes legally. Southeast Asian countries, however, at this stage lack the capacity to monitor every sea and air passage; the vast size of the maritime zone makes it difficult to make a strong legal claim based on well-monitored accumulated violations.

Finally, Southeast Asian countries will always face a tough decision between the United States and China, with domestic politicization remaining a challenge. Japan's strategic role and its importance is that it can offer a low-risk hedge that prevents Southeast Asian countries from being drawn into a zero-sum game between the United States and China.

RECOMMENDATIONS FOR JAPAN'S SOUTHEAST ASIA POLICY AND THE U.S.-JAPAN ALLIANCE IN SOUTHEAST ASIA

Southeast Asia's core interest is maintaining its political and economic stability. Japan's strategy should be first, to meet Southeast Asia's interests; second, to strengthen Southeast Asia; and third, to reinforce its position as a reliable and legitimate partner for Southeast Asia. It is critical that Japan and the United States actively engage Southeast Asia. The expectation that Southeast Asia will "risk hedge" must be the baseline for designing a strategy toward Southeast Asia. Stronger triangular ties among Southeast Asia, Japan, and the United States are fundamental to effective risk hedging. East Asia is undergoing a subtle competition for legitimacy and legality, in addition to the military and economic power balance. "Just showing up" at multilateral conferences such as EAS and APEC is not good enough anymore; setting the political agenda is the real battleground. In so doing, there are four areas in which the United States and Japan should further commit themselves:

I.   Economic Resilience

- Macroeconomic performance in Southeast Asia continues to rise and impress the world, but Gini coefficients are also rising. In order to lessen economic disparities while sustaining growth, the United States and Japan should first support economic reforms and second support private infrastructure development. Supporting private investment in key transportation projects will be a catalyst for regional development in Southeast Asia. Supporting underdeveloped zones would not only balance the economy but also help to stabilize local politics.

- Supporting middle-class expansion by promoting advanced skilled labor will help to capitalize on broader economic opportunities. Japanese companies are in an especially good position to meet the expectations of South-east Asian countries facing this challenge, due to Japan's capacity-building experience as well as its manufacturing and production standards. This would not only establish the basis for a value-added economy in Southeast Asia, but it would also encourage a consumption market and liberal democracy, creating a win-win for Southeast Asia and Japan.

2.   *Political Resilience*

- Japan's biggest strength is the trust it has cultivated in Southeast Asia over 40 years. To ameliorate Southeast Asian countries' fear of being trapped between the United States and China, Japan needs to explain that its goal in Southeast Asia is not containing China, but rather balancing and stabilizing Southeast Asia by keeping its policy options open. Diplomatically, Japan needs to expand dialogue channels to lower tensions with China, as Indonesia's president requested in December 2013, while strengthening its alliance with the United States.

- Southeast Asian political reform is increasingly dependent on the judiciary; as we have learned in Thailand, a trusted judiciary is crucial for sustaining political stability. Thus, building judicial networks will be fundamental to creating common ground on the rule of law, regardless of the differences in political and legal structures. Japan and the United States could both play critical roles in establishing such a judicial network.

- Political stability cannot be accomplished without tackling social disparity. It is high time for Southeast Asian states to design upgraded medical and taxation systems. Japan's healthcare system could be a good reference point, helping Southeast Asia to enhance both the taxation and medical systems.

- Civil society is also critical. Southeast Asia has recovered from the Asian financial crisis and has enjoyed economic growth for more than a decade. There is a growing civil society across Southeast Asia composed of informed and civically minded people. Fostering civil society is vital to the future of Southeast Asia; this includes the freedom of press, rule of law, and democracy. Such efforts require U.S. support together with help from regional allies and partners that share these common principles. The United States has the power to set the agenda, so enhancing the skills and capabilities of hitherto unconnected counterparts should be a priority.

- One of the most powerful values that the United States is identified with is liberty. The promotion of human rights is also important. Japan can raise the value of resilience, which is ultimately a humanitarian value. The U.S.-Japan alliance thus is a complementary alliance of human rights promotion and humanitarian relief.

3. *Environmental Resilience*

- Japan and Southeast Asia share the challenge of managing severe natural disasters such as tsunamis, earthquakes, floods, and volcanoes. Establishing a network of resilient urban societies based on shared values of environmental stewardship and disaster prevention is fundamental to sustainable growth in Asia. Improved urban planning, urban infrastructure, disaster management, and transportation development are necessary to increase resilience against natural disasters. Japan should invite those with expertise in these fields to assist with enhancing Southeast Asia's resilience for the sake of not only Southeast Asia, but also foreign partners. Energy-saving and environmentally respectful governance is also critical in terms of political accountability and stability. This will create a new standard that will nurture common societal values in the region.

4.   *Security Resilience*

- Southeast Asia needs enhanced radar and surveillance systems at sea, in the air, and underwater. Capacity building is needed in monitoring operations and analysis, as demonstrated by the challenging Malaysia Airlines search effort. In the short term, especially until a code of conduct is agreed upon, it is particularly important that Japan help to enhance Filipino and Vietnamese maritime security to stand firm against Chinese fait accompli tactics.

- Japan, together with the United States, should take diplomatic steps to implement the United Nations Convention on the Law of the Sea (UNCLOS). It is also high time that the United States ratifies UNCLOS to gain the legal high ground in Asia's political dynamics.

- The U.S.-Japan alliance should be used as a common platform for information sharing on maritime activities and China's new East China Sea Air Defense Identification Zone. Updated maritime traffic rules and maritime pollution-monitoring mechanisms should include all parties in the South China Sea and East China Sea.

- Enhancing the role and function of the ADMM-Plus is vital as it offers the best channel for defense ministers to sit together on a regular basis. Establishing a multilayer dialogue is crucial to the ADMM-Plus. Cooperation should include: regional antipiracy, humanitarian assistance and disaster relief, sustainable fisheries, maritime law, and maritime communication. This multilayered approach would create a limited but important opportunity to convert the South China Sea from an area of potential conflict into an area of cooperation. This inclusive mechanism with ASEAN at the helm should help China create a space to show that China's rise contributes to the common good of all.

- Humanitarian assistance and disaster relief (HA/DR) with Southeast Asian partners, Korea, and the United States should also be expanded. China is welcome to join, which would make for a great platform for future cooperation.

In conclusion, the U.S.-Japan alliance could offer what is needed in Southeast Asia and vice versa. Both alliance partners agree on the strategic importance of Southeast Asia, and thus should not hesitate to cooperate in securing stability and sustainable growth in that region. Southeast Asia is now entering the golden decade of its demographic dividend. This era has already passed in Japan, China, Taiwan, and South Korea. Thus, if we are to expect a prosperous Asia in the decades ahead, Southeast Asia is the key to the promising path. Pursuing areas of common ground with Southeast Asia's rising middle class, establishing a resilient social system in the region, and confronting numerous common challenges (such as natural disaster and other nontraditional security issues) are crucial for Southeast Asia's future as well as that of Japan and the United States. ∎

INDEX

Note: Page numbers followed by *f* and *t* indicate figures and tables, respectively.

A

A2/AD strategy. *See* Anti-access/area denial (A2/AD) strategy
Abduction issue, 67, 71
Abe, Shinzo, 20, 22*t*, 30
    ASEAN-focused diplomacy, 112–113
    policy of proactive pacifism, 1–2, 51
    strategic diplomacy, 50–51, 56
    strategic vision of, 49–50
Abenomics, 50
    three arrows of, 1–2, 50
Acquisition and Cross-Servicing Agreement (ACSA), 74, 77
Active defense, Chinese, 39–40
Air Defense Identification Zone (ADIZ), Chinese, 22*t*, 35, 40, 68, 72, 126
Air-Sea Battle (ASB), 47–49, 56, 57–58
Aizawa, Nobuhiro, 4–5
Akutsu, Hiroyasu, 4
Alaska, oil exports to Japan, 91–92
Amphibious assault vehicles
    Japanese, 54–55
    joint development of, by U.S. and Japan, 58–59
Anti-access/area denial (A2/AD) strategy, Chinese, 35–36, 36–43, 46–49, 56
    Air-Sea Battle and, 47–49
    implications of, 41–43

    offshore control and, 48–49
Antiship ballistic missile (ASBM) defense
    Chinese, 38–39
    joint development of, by U.S. and Japan, 59
Antiship weapons, Chinese, 38–41
Antisubmarine warfare (ASW), Japanese capabilities for, 53
Arab Spring, 85–86
ASEAN-Japan Commemorative Summit, 112–113
Asia-Pacific Economic Cooperation (APEC), 112, 114
    and international energy market, 99
Assertiveness. *See also* Chinese assertiveness
    reactive, 8–9, 26
Association of Southeast Asian Nations (ASEAN), 2, 112
    and China, 120–121
    Defense Ministers' Meeting Plus (ADMM-Plus), 126–127
        Humanitarian Assistance and Disaster Relief and Military Medicine Exercise, 121
    Economic Community, 116
    economic resilience in, 116
    Japan's role in, 5, 50–51, 112–113, 121–122
    and maritime order, effects on energy security, 100–101

Regional Forum, 121
Association of Southeast Asian
Nations+3 (ASEAN+3), 112
    and international energy
    market, 99
Association of Southeast Asian
Nations+6 (ASEAN+6), 112
Aung San Suu Kyi, 117
Australia
    and Asia's democratic security
    diamond, 50
    and Japan, security agreement, 2
    and stability in Indo-Asia-
    Pacific, 75
    U.S. Marines in, 44
    and U.S. naval basing, 44
    and U.S. rebalancing in Asia,
    44, 45
Aviation, in Southeast Asia, 112, 119

B
Ballistic missile(s). *See also* Antiship
ballistic missile (ASBM)
defense; Intercontinental
ballistic missiles (ICBMs)
    North Korean, 67–68
Ballistic missile defense (BMD),
67, 68
    Japan's role in, 70–71
    Japan–U.S.–South Korea
    trilateral cooperation for, 76–78
Basic Energy Plan (BEP), Japanese,
79, 108–109
Beijing consensus, 10
Bilateral Commission on Civil
Nuclear Cooperation, U.S.-Japan, 107
Blake, William, 7, 32
Bower, Ernest, 5
Brunei, maritime challenges from
China, 119

C
Cambodia
    and China, relations between,
    31, 120
    economic development in, 116
    political stability in, 117
Carbon emissions, reduction, 98
Carrier killer, shore-based, Chinese, 38
Center for Strategic and
International Studies

(CSIS), visiting scholars,
2–3
Cha, Victor, 4
Chen Shui-bian, 30
China
    anti-access/area denial (A2/
    AD) strategy. See Anti-access/
    area denial (A2/AD) strategy,
    Chinese
    coastal defense, 37–38
    contemporary politics, 17–19
    core interests of, 10
    cultivation of patriotism
    (*aiguozhuyi*), 11–12, 13f, 18–19
    defense budget of, 11
    diplomatic and political
    pressure on Japan, 8
    direct and indirect rivals of,
    23–24, 24t–25t
    economic expansion, 11, 17
    energy security concerns, 101
    foreign policy, 17
    foreign relations, cycles of
    deterioration/amelioration, 3,
    10, 17–23
    gross domestic product (GDP)
    of, 11
    independent foreign policy of
    peace (*dulizizhu de hepingwaijiao*), 17
    and Japan, relations between,
    Chinese politics and, 18–21,
    21t–22t
    maritime expansion, 8, 14–15,
    49, 56
    maritime law enforcement
    strategies, 40–41
    maritime strategy, 3–4, 42
    and North Korea, relations
    between, 61, 64, 68
    nuclear arsenal, 42
    People's Liberation Army Navy.
    See PLAN
    perception of Japan since 2007, 8
    position on Diaoyu Islands
    (*Diaoyudao*), 11–14, 13f
    provocations vs attempts to
    amend ties with Japan (2012–
    2013), 20–21, 21t–22t
    rising power trend and, 3
    and South Korea
        history between,
        "containment" of, 75–76

relations between, 62, 68
strategic framing of Japan, 9
strategic relations with its
neighbors, 27–33
strategic rivalry, 3
and United States, relations
between, 23–25, 24*t*, 42
use of trade as weapon, 120
as world's second-largest
economy, 11
China Marine Surveillance, 15
Chinese assertiveness
cycles of deterioration/
amelioration hypothesis, 3, 10,
17–23
policy implications of, 28–29
definition of, 8
as reactive, 9, 26
redefinition of strategic rivals
hypothesis, 10, 23–27
policy implications of, 29–31
rising trend hypothesis, 10–17
policy implications of, 27–28
since 2009, 1–3, 8
territorial and maritime claims
and, 43
U.S. rebalancing policy and, 10,
36, 43–49
Climate change, damage from,
mitigation, 97–98
CLM countries, economic
development in, 116
Coal-fired power plants, 97
and Japan's energy security
policy, 84
Coast Guard
Chinese, 41
Japanese, 50, 55–56
Colby, Elbridge, 48
Collective self-defense right,
Japan's, 69–70
Communist Party of China, direct
and indirect rivals of, 23–24,
24*t*–25*t*
Confidence building, Sino-Japanese,
52, 59
Cooper, Zack, 3
Counter-intervention strategy,
Chinese, 42
Crisis communication/
management, Sino-Japanese, 52, 59

D
Dai Bingguo, 20
Democratic Party, of Japan, 1
Democratic security diamond, 50
Deterrence, 52, 56. *See also* Air-Sea
Battle (ASB); War-at-sea strategy
enhancement/extension, 69–70
on Korean peninsula, 75
in Northeast Asia, 75
against North Korea, 66, 76
cooperation among multiple
U.S. allies for, 78
by denial, 66
by punishment, 66
North Korea's belligerence and,
65–66, 65*t*
Diaoyu Islands *(Diaoyudao). See also*
Senkaku Islands
China's position on, 11–14, 13*f*
Disaster relief, in Southeast Asia, 118
Dynamic defense, 53
Dynamic joint defense force, 36,
52–56

E
Earthquake (3-11), 108
energy supply after, 101–102
and Japan's energy security,
85, 86
East Asia, strategic conditions in,
27–33
East Asia Summit (EAS), 112
East China Sea. *See also* Air Defense
Identification Zone (ADIZ), Chinese
activity in, information sharing on, 126
China's assertive engagement
with, 12–15, 22t, 23, 26, 35, 42,
58, 59
Chinese claims on, 40
Chinese UAV (drone) flight over,
22*t*
Japanese naval strategy for,
53, 56
political tensions in, energy
security and, 86
U.S. presence in, 45
Eastern Europe, destabilization, 46
Emergency response
energy supply in, government
decisionmaking and, 101–102
nationwide and and interagency

exercises in, 102–103
Energy conservation, in Japan, 84
Energy demand
    Asian, trends in, 86
    international, factors affecting, 86
Energy imports, Japanese, and consumer burden, 88
Energy intensity, Japan's, 84
Energy market, free and open trade in, 98–99
Energy pricing references, diversification, 95–96
Energy resilience, 80–85
    adverse events and, 83–84
    components of, 80
    and crisis management, 84
    and impact mitigation, 84–85
    Japan's, 4, 108–109, 109t
        and commercial benefit for private firms, 105
        and economic competitiveness, 104–105
        energy supply and, 85–87
        enhancement, policy items for, 87–105, 87t
        impact mitigation in, enhancement, policy items for, 87t
        prompt recovery from, enhancement, policy items for, 87t
        U.S.-Japan alliance and, 105–108
    and risk management, 84
    three pillars of, 4
Energy security policy, Japan's, 84, 108–109, 109t
Energy sources, Japanese policy on, 79
Energy stockpiles, mobilizing, 103–104
Energy supply
    government decisionmaking and, 101–102
    international, geopolitical factors affecting, 85–86
    Japan's
        diversification of, 90–93
        risks to, 86–87
        vulnerabilities of, 86–87

Exclusive economic zone (EEZ), Chinese, 40
External balancing strategy, Abe's, 2, 50, 56–57

F

Five Dragons, 41
Fleet-in-being, 41, 56
    Chinese, 39–41
    definition, 36–37
    historical perspective on, 39
    as sea-denial strategy, 40
Fleet-in-dispersal, U.S., 45
Fortress fleet, 41, 56
    China's, 37–39
    definition, 36–37
    offensive role, 39
France, as indirect rival of China, 24t
Fravel, M. Taylor, 8
Freedom of navigation program, U.S.-Japanese, 58
Fukushima Daiichi Nuclear Power Plant accident, 85, 86, 108

G

G-2 dilemma, in South Korea, 74
G-8, and international energy market, 99
G-20, and international energy market, 99
Glaser, Bonnie, 3
Global financial crisis (2008), 10
Gray zone scenarios, China and Japan in, 53, 55–57, 59
Greenhouse gas (GHGs) emissions, controlling, 97–98
Gregson, Wallace (Chip), 4
Guam, U.S. Marines in, 44
Guidelines for Defense Cooperation, U.S.-Japan, and space/cyberspace security, 68

H

Hainan EP-3 incident (2001), 40
Hainan Island, Chinese underwater submarine base on, 42
Hammes, T. X., 4, 48
Harold, Scott W., 8
Hawaii, U.S. Marines in, 44
Helicopter-equipped destroyers (DDHs), Japanese, 53
Herbert, Arthur (Earl of Torrington), 37, 39

Hiebert, Murray, 5
Hirihito (Japanese Emperor), visit to Beijing (1992), 18
Hughes, Wayne, 49
Hu Jintao, 17, 18–20
Humanitarian assistance/disaster relief, in Southeast Asia, 118, 125, 127
Hurricane Katrina, energy supply after, 99
Hurricane Rita, energy supply after, 99
Hu Yaobang, 18, 19
Hypersonic glide vehicle, Chinese, 42–43

I

Incidents at Sea (INCSEA) Agreement, China and, 52
India
    and Asia's democratic security diamond, 50
    as direct rival of China, 25, 25*t*
    and Japan, security agreement, 2
    and stability in Indo-Asia-Pacific, 75
Indonesia
    economic development in, 116
    economic resilience in, enhancement, 115
Intelligence, surveillance, and reconnaissance (ISR)
    Japanese capabilities for, 53
    Japan–U.S.–South Korea trilateral cooperation for, 76–78
Intercontinental ballistic missiles (ICBMs), Chinese, 42
Internal balancing strategy, Abe's, 2, 50, 56–57
International Crisis Group, concept of reactive assertiveness, 8–9
International Energy Agency, and international energy market, 99
Island chain(s)
    first, 35
        China's maritime strategy in, 38
        deterrence of China in, 3
        sea-denial in, 57
        U.S. Marines in, 45
    second, China's maritime strategy in, 38

J

Jang Song Thaek, 61, 64
Japan
    ASEAN-focused diplomacy, 112–113
    and China
        confidence building, 52, 59
        crisis communication/management, 52, 59
        maritime consultation, 52
    as direct rival of China, 25*t*, 26–27
    and dynamic joint defense force, 36, 52–56
    engagement strategy for China, 51–52
    and North Korea, abduction issue, 67, 71
    postwar economic revitalization, 1
    proactive security role for, 56–57, 57–58. *See also* Proactive pacifism
    response and deterrence capabilities, enhancement, 70
    role with assertive China, 27–29
    and South Korea
        common strategic vision and objectives, 74–75
        common values, 74–75
        joint security declaration, 75
        relations between, 62
    and stability in Indo-Asia-Pacific, 75
    strategic alliance with U.S., India, and Australia, 50
    as strategic rival for China, 28–31
    and United States, bilateral defense guidelines, 2, 36, 57–59
Japan Ground Self-Defense Force (JGSDF), 54
Japan Maritime Self-Defense Force (JMSDF), 53
    Aegis system, 69, 71
Japan–ROK joint naval exercises, 72, 73*t*
Japan–ROK–U.S. joint naval exercises, 72, 73*t*
Japan Self-Defense Forces (JSDF), 53
Japan–South Korea General Security of Military Information Agreement

(GSOMIA), 72, 74, 77
Japan-Taiwan fishery agreement, 59
Japan-U.S. Security Treaty, 64
Japan–U.S.–South Korea trilateral
security cooperation, 4, 68, 72,
76–78
Jerdén, Björn, 9–10
Jiang Zemin, 18, 19
Johnson, Chris, 3
Johnston, Alistair Iain, 9

K

Kim Il Sung, 62
Kim Jong Un, 61, 62–63
Kline, Jeffrey, 49
Kobayashi, Yoshikazu, 4
Koizumi, Junichiro, 19–20
Korean Peninsula Energy
Development Organization (KEDO),
77
Korean War, 24*t*, 25
Kotani, Tetsuo, 3–4
Kuomintang, as direct rival of
China, 24, 24*t*, 26
Kyoto Protocol, 97–98

L

Laos, economic development in, 116
Lee Teng-hui, 30
Legal warfare, as Chinese sea-denial
strategy, 40, 58
Le Mière, Christian, 45
Liberal Democratic Party, of Japan, 1
Liquified natural gas (LNG)
exports to Japan, from U.S.,
105–106
imports from North America,
93
and Japan's energy security
policy, 84
from Middle East, 90
for power generation, 96–97
pricing, 95–96
sources, for Japan,
diversification, 93, 95f
Littoral combat ships (LCCs)
joint development of, by U.S.
and Japan, 59
United States, 49
Pacific deployment, 44
Liu Huaqing, 38
Luttwak, Edward, 27

M

Mahan, Alfred Thayer, 37
Malaysia
economic development in, 116
economic resilience in,
enhancement, 115
maritime challenges from
China, 119
Mao Zedong, 39
Marines-in-dispersal, in Asia,
45–46, 56
Maritime law enforcement
asymmetric power
relationships in Southeast Asia
and, 119
Chinese strategies, 40–41, 119
Maritime order, international
and energy security, 100–101
and Southeast Asian security, 119
Matsuda, Yasuhiro, 3
Middle East
geopolitical uncertainties in,
85–86
liquified natural gas from, 90
oil from, 85–86, 92–93, 94f
oil supply from, 90–93
United States in, 45–46
Military Maritime Consultative
Agreement (MMCA), U.S.-China, 52
Myanmar
economic development in, 116
political stability in, 116–117

N

Nakano, Jane, 4
Nakasone, Yasuhiro, 19
Nansei Islands, 36
civilian/commercial airfields, 54
defense of, 52–56, 57
military airfields, 54
National Defense Program
Guidelines (NDPG), Japanese, 36,
50, 52, 61, 69, 70, 71
National Security Council (NSC)
of Japan, 2, 36, 50, 61
Japanese, 69
National Security Strategy (NSS),
Japanese, 36, 50–51, 61, 69
articulation of Japan's North
Korea strategy, 66–67
Natural disasters
and Japan's energy security,
86–87

resilience against,
enhancement, 125–126
in Southeast Asia, management
of, 118
Near Seas
allied maritime and air
surveillance in, 58
Chinese assertive maritime
strategy in, 35, 43
non-Chinese surveillance
activity in, 40
PLAN activity in, 40
U.S. presence in, 45
NIA/D$_3$, 47
Noda, Yoshihiko, 1
North Korea
ballistic missile threat, 67–68
belligerence of, Japan's policy
response to, 65–66, 65t
and China, relations between,
61, 64, 68
Japan's security policy for,
64–67, 66–67
Japan's strategy for, 4
and Japan–U.S.–South Korea
trilateral security cooperation,
76–78
missile development program,
63, 66, 67, 76
nuclear weapons doctrine, 63
nuclear weapons program,
62–63, 66–67, 68
position as nuclear weapons
state, 64
recent developments in, 61–64
Nuclear energy
Japanese policy on, 79
and Japan's energy security
policy, 84
safety myth and, 85, 89
U.S.-Japan bilateral cooperation
and, 107
Nuclear Power Cooperation
Agreement, U.S.-Japan, 107
Nuclear power plant safety, in
Japan, 88–90
nationwide and and interagency
exercises in, 102–103
public acceptance of and
confidence in, 88–89
regulatory framework and,
88–89
and zero-risk concept, 89–90

Nuclear Regulatory Authority
(NRA), Japanese, 88–89

O
Obama administration
and fiscal policy, 46
and Middle East, 45–46
rebalancing policy in Asia,
44–46
Offshore control, and Chinese A2/
AD strategy, 48–49
Oil
and Japan's energy security
policy, 84
for power generation, 97
Oil stockpiles
for commercial purposes, 104
Japanese, 84
Japanese and Middle Eastern
joint arrangements for, 103–104
mobilizing, 103–104
test releases, 104
Oil supply
Asian
imports for, 86
trends in, 92–93, 94f
Japan's
diversification of, 90–93
geopolitical factors affecting,
85–86
Okinawa
Chinese submarine near, 22t
U.S. Marines in, 45

P
Paramilitary maritime coercion,
Chinese, 41, 49, 56
Patriotism *(aiguozhuyi)*, state-led
invocation of, in China, 11–12, 13f,
18–19
People's Liberation Army Navy. *See*
PLAN
Philippines
China's relations with, 9, 120
as direct rival of China, 25t,
26–27
economic resilience in,
enhancement, 115
humanitarian assistance/
disaster relief in, 118
and Japan, ties between, 2, 28
maritime challenges from

135

China, 119
    maritime security of, 126
    role with assertive China, 27–29
    and United States, ties between,
    28, 120
    and U.S. rebalancing in Asia, 45
Philippine Sea, Japanese naval
strategy for, 53
PLAN, 38–39, 56
    as hybrid of fortress fleet and
    fleet-in-being, 41
    offshore active defense, 39–40
    strategically defensive role,
    41–42
    and strategic counteroffensive, 42
    tactically offensive role, 41–42
PLA Navy. See PLAN
Power generation, energy mix for,
optimizing, 96–97
Proactive pacifism, 1–2, 51
Proliferation Security Initiative
(PSI), 77, 78
Pumphrey, David, 4
Pyongyang Declaration, Japan-
North Korea, 65, 67

Q
Quadrennial Defense Review (QDR)
(2014), 46, 49

R
Reactive assertiveness, 8–9, 26. See
also Chinese assertiveness
Rebalancing policy. See United
States, rebalancing policy
Renewable energy, 96
Republic of Korea (ROK)
    and China, relations between,
    31, 68
    Chinese charm offensive
    toward, 62, 74
    as direct rival of China, 24t
    G-2 dilemma, 74
    and Japan
        history between, 2, 62, 68,
        75–76
        joint naval exercises, 72, 73t
        and pragmatism over
        emotionalism, 75–76
        security cooperation, 71–76
    and Japan's collective self-
    defense right, 69–70

and Japan–U.S.–South Korea
    trilateral security cooperation,
    76–78
    trilateral cooperation with U.S.
    and Japan, 4, 68, 72
Republic of Korea (South Korea)-
China honeymoon, 62, 74
Resilience, 80. See also Energy
resilience
    in business management, 81–82
    in civil engineering, 80–82
    common aspects across
    disciplines, 82
    definition of, 80–82
    economic, 81, 82
        in Southeast Asia,
        enhancement, 114–116,
        123–124
    environmental, in Southeast
    Asia, enhancement, 118, 125–126
    essential elements of, 83, 83f
    Japan's, 114
    in macroeconomics, 81
    in mathematics, 80
    political, in Southeast Asia,
    enhancement, 116–118, 124–125
    as proactive, 82
    psychological, 81
    security, in Southeast Asia,
    enhancement, 118–122, 126–127
    in Southeast Asia, 114
        enhancement, 114–127
    and time needed to recover,
    82–83
Rice, Susan, 46
Risk hedging, 52
    in Southeast Asia, 112, 123
Russia. See also Soviet Union
    and China, ties between, 29
    oil supply to Asian markets, 92
Russian Navy, early 20th c., 37
Russo-Japanese War of 1904–05,
37–39
Ryuku Islands, Chinese naval
vessels crossing, frequency of, 12, 14

S
Safety, Anshin and Anzen concepts
of, 88
Safety myth, and nuclear energy,
85, 89
Scarborough Shoal, 120

standoff over, 41
Scobell, Andrew, 8
Sea-denial strategy, Chinese, 40
Sea lines of communication
(SLOCs), and energy security,
100–101
Senkaku Islands. *See also* Diaoyu
Islands *(Diaoyudao)*
    China's assertive engagement
    with, 12–14, 16*f*, 19–20, 21*t*, 22*t*,
    25, 25*t*, 30–31, 41, 59
    Chinese fishing boat and
    Japan Coast Guard patrol boat
    collision near (2010), 20
    defense of, 57
    Japanese purchase of three of
    (2012), 20–21
Sento Islands. *See* Diaoyu Islands
(Diaoyudao)
Shipping, in Southeast Asia, 112
Singapore
    economic development in, 116
    economic resilience in,
    enhancement, 115
Six-Party Talks, 64
South China Sea
    activity in, information sharing
    on, 126
    China's assertive engagement
    with, 9, 23, 25*t*, 26, 35, 42, 58,
    119
    Chinese claims on, 40
    maritime security in, and
    regional security, 119
    political tensions in, energy
    security and, 86
    U.S. presence in, 45
Southeast Asia
    aviation in, 112, 119
    civil society in, 125
    consumer market in, 115–116
    disaster management in, 118
    diversification (risk hedging)
    in, 112
    economic disparity in, 116,
    123–124
    economic growth in, 111, 112,
    123–124
    economic resilience in,
    enhancement, 114–116, 123–124
    environmental resilience in,

enhancement, 118, 125–126
    ethnic issues in, 118
    geopolitical significance of,
    111–112
    gross domestic product (GDP), 111
    humanitarian assistance/disaster
    relief in, 118, 125, 127
    Japanese investment in, 115
    and Japan's regional strategy,
    4–5, 111–114
    Japan's role in, 113–114
        recommendations for, 123–127
    Japan-U.S. alliance and, 111–127
        recommendations for, 123–127
    liberal democracy in, 117–118
    middle class in, 115, 123
    political resilience in,
    enhancement, 116–118, 124–125
    political stability in, 124
        judicial system and, 117, 124
    as production base, 115–116
    regional development in, 123
    resilience in, 114
        enhancement, 114–127
    security resilience in,
    enhancement, 118–122, 126–127
    and shipping, 112
    strategic meaning of, 113–114
    U.S. role in, 125
South Korea. *See* Republic of Korea
(ROK)
Southwestern Island chain. *See*
Nansei Islands
Soviet Union. *See also* Russia
    as direct rival of China, 24*t*, 25,
    25*t*, 26
    as indirect rival of China, 24*t*, 25*t*
Space/cyberspace security, North
Korean threat and, 68
Spear and shield, 57–58
Stability-instability paradox, 43, 56,
76
Strategic mobility, U.S.–Japanese,
enhancement of, 58
Submarine fleet
    Chinese, 40, 42
    Japanese, 54
Surveillance. *See also* Intelligence,
surveillance, and reconnaissance
(ISR)
    allied, in Near Seas, 58

Japanese, in maritime zones,
  53, 122
Swaine, Michael, 8

T

Taiwan
  and China, relations between,
    9, 29, 30
  China's claim to, 23
  as direct rival of China, 24, 24*t*,
    25, 25*t*, 26
  role with assertive China, 27
  ties with Japan and U.S., 59
Tan Shwe, 117
Thailand
  economic development in, 116
  economic resilience in,
    enhancement, 115
  political stability in, 117
    judicial system and, 124
  and U.S. rebalancing in Asia, 45
Thein Sein, 116–117
Thermal power generation sources,
  optimizing, 96–97
Tiananmen Square (1989), 18
Tohoku Great Earthquake, 118
Tokyo-Guam-Taiwan (TGT)
  Triangle, Japanese naval strategy
  for, 53
Trans-Pacific Partnership (TPP),
  2, 59
  and international energy
    market, 99
Trilateral Policy Oversight and
  Coordination Group (TCOG), 77

U

Ukraine, Russian intervention in, 46
UN Convention on the Law of the
  Sea (UNCLOS), 51, 120–121, 126
United States
  allies of, cooperation among, in
    Asia-Pacific, 78
  Asian interests, 43–44
  and Asia's democratic security
    diamond, 50
  and China, relations between,
    42
  defense assets, fiscal
    constraints on, 46
  as direct rival of China, 23–24,
    24*t*, 26

energy exports, 106
engagement in East Asia, 28–30
as indirect rival of China, 24*t*,
  25*t*
and Japan
  bilateral defense guidelines,
    2, 36, 57–59
  deterrence of China's
    maritime strategy, 3–4
and Japan's collective self-
  defense right, 69–70
and Japan–U.S.–South Korea
  trilateral security cooperation,
  76–78
naval posture in Asia, 44–46, 56
net oil imports, trends in, 90–91
oil export restrictions, 91–92
oil supply from, 90–93
as Pacific nation, 43
presence in Northeast Asia,
  Japan and, 75
rebalancing policy, 10, 36,
  43–49, 56, 106
  Asian concerns about U.S.
    commitment to, 46
  role in Japan–South Korea
    security cooperation, 72
  role with assertive China, 27–30
  sea-control fleet, in Pacific,
    44–46, 56
  as strategic rival for China,
    28–33
United States Marines, dispersion,
  44
U.S.-Japan Defense Guidelines, 2,
  36, 57–59
USNS *Impeccable,* 40–41
USS *Cowpens,* 35, 40, 52
USS *Kitty Hawk,* Chinese attack
  submarine and, 40
USSR. *See* Soviet Union

V

Vietnam
  China's relations with, 9
  as direct rival of China, 25, 25*t*
  economic development in, 116
  maritime challenges from
    China, 119
  maritime security of, 126
  role with assertive China, 27–28

and United States, ties between,
120
and U.S. rebalancing in Asia, 45

W

War-at-sea strategy, 57
and Chinese aggression, 49,
55–56
War of the League of Augsburg, 39
Weapons of mass destruction
(WMD), North Korean development
of, deterrence of, 75
Wen Jiabao, address to National Diet
of Japan (4/12/2007), 7, 8

X

Xi Jinping, 16–17, 19, 22*t*, 42

Y

Yamaguchi, Natsuo, 22*t*
Yasukuni Shrine, 20
Yellow Sea
Chinese claims on, 40
U.S. presence in, 45
Yoshida, Shigeru, 1
Yoshida Doctrine, 1
Yudhoyono, Susilo Bambang, 114

ABOUT THE EDITORS & AUTHORS

Michael J. Green is senior vice president for Asia and Japan Chair at the Center for Strategic and International Studies (CSIS) and an associate professor at the Edmund A. Walsh School of Foreign Service at Georgetown University. He served on the staff of the National Security Council (NSC) from 2001 through 2005, first as director for Asian affairs, with responsibility for Japan, Korea, Australia, and New Zealand, and then as special assistant to the president for national security affairs and senior director for Asia, with responsibility for East Asia and South Asia. Before joining the NSC staff, he was senior fellow for East Asian security at the Council on Foreign Relations; director of the Edwin O. Reischauer Center and the Foreign Policy Institute, and an assistant professor at the School of Advanced International Studies (SAIS) at Johns Hopkins University; research staff member at the Institute for Defense Analyses; and senior adviser on Asia in the Office of the Secretary of Defense. He also worked in Japan on the staff of a member of the National Diet.

Zack Cooper is a fellow with the Japan Chair at the Center for Strategic and International Studies, where he focuses on Asian security issues. He is also a doctoral candidate in security studies at Princeton University's Woodrow Wilson School. Prior to joining CSIS, Mr. Cooper worked as a research fellow at the Center for Strategic and Budgetary Assessments. He previously served on the White House staff as assistant to the deputy national security adviser for combating terrorism. He also worked as a civil servant in the Pentagon, first as a foreign affairs specialist and then as a special assistant to the principal deputy under secretary of defense for policy.

* * *

Nobuhiro Aizawa is an associate professor at the Graduate School of Social and Cultural Studies at Kyushu University and a visiting scholar with the Japan Chair at the Center for Strategic and International Studies in Washington, D.C.

Hiroyasu Akutsu is a senior fellow and professor at the National Institute for Defense Studies (NIDS) in Tokyo and a visiting scholar with the Japan Chair at the Center for Strategic and International Studies in Washington, D.C.

Yoshikazu Kobayashi is a senior economist and manager of the Oil Group of the Institute of Energy Economics, Japan (IEEJ), and a visiting scholar with the Japan Chair at the Center for Strategic and International Studies in Washington, D.C.

Tetsuo Kotani is a senior research fellow at the Japan Institute of International Affairs (JIIA) and a visiting scholar with the Japan Chair at the Center for Strategic and International Studies in Washington, D.C.

Yasuhiro Matsuda is a professor of international politics at the University of Tokyo Interfaculty Initiative in Information Studies, a professor at the Institute for Advanced Studies on Asia, and a visiting scholar with the Japan Chair at the Center for Strategic and International Studies in Washington, D.C.

ABOUT CSIS

For over 50 years, the Center for Strategic and International Studies (CSIS) has worked to develop solutions to the world's greatest policy challenges. Today, CSIS scholars are providing strategic insights and bipartisan policy solutions to help decisionmakers chart a course toward a better world.

CSIS is a nonprofit organization headquartered in Washington, D.C. The Center's 220 full-time staff and large network of affiliated scholars conduct research and analysis and develop policy initiatives that look into the future and anticipate change.

Founded at the height of the Cold War by David M. Abshire and Admiral Arleigh Burke, CSIS was dedicated to finding ways to sustain American prominence and prosperity as a force for good in the world. Since 1962, CSIS has become one of the world's preeminent international institutions focused on defense and security; regional stability; and transnational challenges ranging from energy and climate to global health and economic integration.

Former U.S. senator Sam Nunn has chaired the CSIS Board of Trustees since 1999. Former deputy secretary of defense John J. Hamre became the Center's president and chief executive officer in 2000.